Cognitive Behavioral Therapy
(2 Manuscripts)

Master Your Brain and Emotions to Overcome Anxiety, Depression and Negative Thoughts

&

An Alternative Treatment for Greater Personal Happiness and Contentment

CONTENTS

Cognitive Behavioral Therapy

Master Your Brain and Emotions to Overcome Anxiety, Depression and Negative Thoughts

ANIVYA PUBLISHING

BILL ANDREWS

INTRODUCTION

THIS IS MY STORY

I've always been shy. I'm not just talking about the kind of garden-variety shyness most people occasionally suffer from. My shyness, to quote the legendary 80s band The Smiths' song "How Soon Is Now," was "criminally vulgar."

I would freeze up – as in physically freeze up. In many cases, I would get scared stiff of having to speak to a crowd of strangers or even meet new people in an unfamiliar place. I didn't want to leave home. That's how bad it was for me.

In fact, every time I had to meet someone new, make a presentation, or otherwise have to be physically in front of people I didn't already know, I would get close to becoming physically sick. Even if I didn't throw up, the physical effects of my shyness really frustrated me. I would get cold sweats. I would feel light headed.

In some cases, I would feel temporarily "deaf." People would talk to me, but I could barely hear what they're saying. In many cases, there were "dead spots" in the words that I was hearing from them. I would try to pass it off by smiling or nodding my head.

Not surprisingly, all these "issues" crippled my social life. And that's only the physical effects of my shyness – the emotional and psychological self-torture that I endured were brutal as well.

Indeed, things got so bad that I thought I would never find anyone to share my life with. My work prospects were very limited since almost all jobs require some sort of interpersonal or public contact. I was at the end of my rope.

I thought I was a hopeless basket case – an irredeemable victim of my own personal neuroses – until I went on a trip with friends to Italy. In between sights at ancient Roman ruins, my best friend told me that my issues were all in my head. He sat me down and broke everything down for me:

- I had a great degree from a top, world-class university.

- I had a great job and a great income – an income most people would love to have.

- I had no debt.

- Everything I possessed, I owned outright.

- I did not have any student debt.

- I was in shape.

- I was not a bad-looking guy.

On and on he went. He was forcing me to look at my life and the stories I chose to believe about myself from a totally different perspective. He was pushing me to look at myself from a perspective I don't usually use. Indeed, most of the time, I was completely unaware of the things I had going for me.

That's when everything changed. My buddy Raul chipped away at the "mental cocoon" I had built for myself. For the longest time, my comfort zone's walls provided me with some measure of comfort. Little did I know, the more I retreated into my fear of people (and rejection), the more the walls of my comfort zone caved in around me. It became my personal mental prison.

After that trip, as I was drinking coffee alone at the company dining hall, I asked myself a very simple question. It turned out to be the key to me turning my life around. I asked myself, "Is this all my life has to offer?" I was staring at the bottom of my empty coffee cup. I could see the droplets of coffee slowly swirling around the coffee cup as I moved it. I kept asking myself that question as I stared at the nearly-empty bottom of my cup. At that point, I made a decision. I made it my personal mission to punch, kick, shoot through, or bulldoze the walls of my personal comfort zone.

Now, I'm able to make presentations to business groups anywhere from Tokyo to Toronto. I'm able to strike up conversations with strangers anywhere – from train stations to airplanes to packed bars. Best of all, I'm able to set them (and myself) at ease.

I also met the love of my life. It took me taking courage and boldly marching out of my comfort zone (and personal shell) for me to meet her... finally!

I was able to do all these because of the one key revelation and personal realization that shot through my brain like a thousand crystal bullets that summer in Rome so many years ago.... I realized I have a tremendous amount of CONTROL over what I choose to FEEL, DO and DEFINE MYSELF AS. In other words, by simply taking ownership of what I choose to believe about myself, I can change my life.

A few years later, I found out that there was actually a scientific name for this personal revelation of mine: cognitive behavioral therapy or CBT.

In this book, I'm going to share with you some practical CBT techniques that can help you overcome fear, limitations, depression, anxiety, emotional over reaction, extreme emotional sensitivity, and other negative states of mind.

Take note: I have consciously written this book in plain English as much as possible. As powerful as the concepts and exercises CBT may bring to the table may be, a lot (too much!) of the professional literature out there seems to be written for psychologists by psychologists, psychiatrists, and other mental health professionals. It seems that they are just speaking to themselves and a lot is lost in translation.

I have taken a different tack. I've written this book using very accessible terms so you can get a clear and actionable set of practices. Apply these to whatever personal issues you're grappling with. That's right. You don't have to have a master's degree or a PhD to understand, put into use, and benefit from the key CBT information contained in this book.

WHO IS THIS BOOK FOR?

This book is for people who are having a tough time dealing with low self-esteem, low self-confidence, social fears, depression, or who constantly think negative and limiting thoughts.

The bottom line? By changing your thought patterns and assumptions, you can make positive changes in your life. These changes help you become a happier, more content person capable of living life with a full sense of well being and contentment.

DISCLAIMER

If you are suffering from a professionally diagnosed mental, emotional, or personality disorder or group of disorders, please make sure you consult with your doctor or primary care provider regarding your treatment options. Continue to take your medications, if any. The information provided in this book is not intended to, nor should be taken as a replacement for whatever professional medical or psychological assistance you're already receiving or thinking of receiving. None of the information presented in this book is intended, nor explicitly or practically positioned, as professional advice or directions or recommendations.

CHAPTER 1:
"IT'S ALL IN YOUR HEAD"- THE CORE OF CBT

My buddy Raul's words ran through my mind for a long time. When he first told me that my shyness was all in my head, my first reaction was, of course, very negative. I was shocked. I was saying, "Who is this guy to tell me that I'm just imagining all these issues? Who is this guy to tell me that, ultimately, I don't really have much of an issue at all?"

I was very resistant. Call it equal parts denial and avoidance, but I really did not want to absorb Raul's summary of what I was going through. But the more I thought about it, the more it sunk in. If it was all in my head, the good news is I can choose to control what gets in my mind. This goes to the heart of CBT.

CBT's fundamental assumptions can be summed up by the following statements:

The way you think distorts your emotional responses to the information you receive from the world around you.

This distorted emotional response produces badly adapted or less-than-ideal decisions or actions from you.

These actions produce negative or less-than-positive results, which further reinforces your negative thinking.

In short, if you're struggling with low self-esteem, low self-confidence, negative thoughts, extreme sensitivity, crushing fears, social insecurity, and other issues, it's because you are stuck in a vicious cycle. You remain trapped in a cycle of self-reinforcing emotional states, choices, and reactions. The lousier you feel, the worse your decisions. Your decisions then make you feel even worse. And on and on it goes.

In fact, a lot of people get so trapped in this pattern for so long that they think that this is completely natural. Many even think this negative state is 'the way things should be'. A lot of people think that being negative is part of who they are. It's easy to feel that there's really nothing you can do to break out of this chain.

In fact, it's quite appealing for many of us to feel that we're victims. Maybe we're victims of the way we were raised as children. Maybe we're victims of our brain chemistry. Whatever the case may be, it's very tempting to think that this internal vicious cycle of negative thoughts and negative actions involves a system that we really did not create and we cannot break out of.

It's quite appealing to feel like a victim because when you assume that role, you take all responsibility off your shoulders. You believe that whatever negativity may be in your life was, inflicted by forces out of your control. You are completely out of the picture and are not responsible. You're just a passive player in this sad movie playing out in front of your eyes-a movie called your life.

Well, it's very easy to think all of the above. In fact, at some level, the conclusions above are quite appealing. Assuming you're a victim or just an unlucky person may make you feel better about the results you're getting with your life. You settle for whatever (often disappointing) results you get until you realize the following:

Realization #1: It's all in your head.

Realization #2: Since it's your head, you have a choice over your thoughts. After all, it's your head.

Realization #3: By being conscious of your thoughts and how you interpret them, you eventually get to the point of being able to change your response.

Realization #4: Change how you judge stimuli, and you change your emotional states.

Realization #5: Change your emotional states and you change the range of physical responses you feel are available to you.

Realization #6: Change your actions and decisions, and you change the results you get or the consequences you have to live with.

Realization #7: Your view of your world, and your personal assumptions, change based on the response you get from the world.

CBT deals with changing personal ideas about yourself so you can filter the world's stimuli in a more empowered and positive way. This will then trigger a chain reaction that enables you to perform and respond to the world in a more optimal way.

Instead of perceiving yourself as some sort of victim of a downward spiral of negative reactions, you can reverse how this spiral plays out with the help of CBT. Instead of sinking deeper and deeper into depression and anxiety, by simply changing how you process stimuli, you can choose a different course of events that lead to better results. How? Simply changing your responses enables you to create an upward spiral where better performance leads to better feelings about yourself. This, in turn leads to greater self-esteem and self-confidence, which leads to even better results. And on and on it goes.

The process above is the key to CBT. There's no magic to it. There is no mysticism involved. There is no magical leap of faith that you need to make. You just need to first become aware of this process. You then claim the tremendous amount of personal power you have over the thoughts you choose to entertain.

CHAPTER 2:
CHANGE HOW YOU PROCESS INFORMATION AND YOU CHANGE YOUR LIFE

Let's get one thing clear: everybody is caught up in a personal roller coaster. We obviously aren't physically on a roller coaster. However, our minds, emotions, and physical actions interact with each other and flow from each other in a way that can definitely feel like a roller coaster ride.

How many times have you found yourself talking to people and somebody says something that you didn't like? Ever felt really small, threatened, and so insecure that ended up saying something that you later regretted? How did the other person react? Maybe they reacted so negatively that you felt even smaller, angrier, bitter, and more powerless than when you began

If this has happened to you, welcome to the club. You are not immune to this very common human experience. This chain of events should give you a good glimpse of how your personal roller coaster works. It seems like it moves automatically. It seems like you don't really have much say on how it all plays out. Things just flash into your mind and all of a sudden you're in some sort of negative emotional state. You then do or say something, things get much worse, and on and on it goes.

The good news is that through CBT, you can finally get off your personal emotional roller coaster. You can take full control of how your emotions interact with how you perceive reality. You then consciously pick among the range of decisions available to you. This leads to you feeling more empowered and effective.

IT'S EASY TO CONFUSE YOUR IDENTITY WITH WHAT YOU DO

When you go to a dinner party and you ask people what they do, most will tell you their occupation. Somebody will say that he or she is a lawyer, another person is a physician, and so on and so forth. As you make introductions or as you think about the people that you've met, it's very easy to identify them by their occupation.

For example, it's very easy for people to mentally file away their friends in terms of their occupations. People routinely say, "My friend Dave is a corporate attorney, my buddy Jenny is a teacher," and so on and so forth. This is how people normally classify themselves and other people. What one does for a living is a proxy or 'short cut' for their identity.

Similarly, outside of formal titles or occupations, we also identify ourselves based on how we normally or routinely act. If you are a person who is very scared of talking to people you don't know, or public speaking, it's easy to identify yourself as shy. After all, that's what you repeatedly do. This raises a lot of troubling questions. What if you tend to repeatedly do something you're not happy with? What if you feel trapped in your routine? What if you wish you would behave another way?

Obviously, if you talk to somebody who feels trapped in a series of thoughts, actions, and decisions that don't make them happy, they will not identify with that pattern. Ideally, people will not say, "Oh, I am a very insecure person" or "I'm an extremely unhappy, depressed person."

Normally, they wouldn't do that. But the problem is, most people feel trapped in their mental, emotional and physical habits. Most people have a fairly passive attitude. Ultimately, they feel that they can't do anything about how they behave. It just happens. It is just part of who they are.

How many times have you talked to friends who are very negative or who have low esteem, and you have, in so many ways, asked them how they view themselves? Chances are quite good that a friend of yours stuck in a negative mental pattern might say to you that that's just who they are. That's part of their personality. This is part of what defines them. The same applies to people who seem to constantly get into arguments all the time or people who create unnecessary drama around themselves.

If this is your attitude towards negative patterns in your life, understand that this 'personal roller coaster ride' doesn't have to be automatic. It doesn't have to play out in front of your eyes with absolutely no input or control from you. It doesn't have to constantly end badly. You can get off the roller coaster you're on.

I know this sounds crazy. It may even sound like it came out of left field. Still, you actually have much more power over your personal reality than you give yourself credit for.

CHANGE YOUR THOUGHTS BY CHANGING WHAT YOU CHOOSE TO PERCEIVE

The first step in getting off the roller coaster is to simply change what you choose to perceive. Believe it or not, in the course of a day, most people pick up hundreds of thousands of sensory signals from the outside world. We pick up things that we see, smell, taste, hear, and touch. All of our senses pick up data from the outside world.

Now, what if I told you that we only choose to perceive a tiny fraction of all that? That's right. We only choose to even become aware of a small subset of all the things that we are constantly picking up.

If you're reading this book right now, your body's picking up all sorts of temperature, scent, light, sounds, and other signals. But most likely, you're just focusing on these words on a white background.

This process happens on auto-pilot you're always choosing what to perceive. These flies in the face of the conclusion a lot of people have regarding their mental and emotional patterns. They feel that things just flash automatically in their mind with no control or input on their part. No.

Thoughts don't just enter your mind. You play a big part in what enters your mind or what you choose to become aware of. You're actually noticing only a fraction of the stimuli you are exposed to.

Understand how this plays out. You're probably asking, "What happens to the rest?" The answer is simple. You chose not to notice them. The reason you're not perceiving them is not because they don't exist. You simply chose not to notice them.

Let me repeat that: It's a choice. You trained yourself through repetition to notice certain things and ignore others. Just like with anything else you learn throughout the course of your life, you can choose to unlearn certain things and learn others.

The reason why you are suffering from anxiety, depression, sadness, low self-confidence, bitterness, unforgiveness, and other negative mental states is because you've trained yourself to notice certain things and not others. When you focus on those things, they are more likely to lead you to negative states of mind.

You choose a set of "raw ingredients" for your mental thought processes that position you to enter negative states of mind. What would happen if you picked a different set of ingredients or raw materials? Maybe you'd have a lot more things to feel positive about? Maybe you'd have a lot more things to be happy about? Still, you habitually choose ingredients that constantly lead you to negative states of mind. What if you can choose to notice different information?

By simply choosing a different subset of the data that you're already processing, your thoughts can switch from negative to positive. Before this happens, you have to first take another step.

CHAPTER 3:
BECOME A BETTER JUDGE OF REALITY

Our thoughts really are a product of two things: the things that we choose to notice and our judgment of what we noticed. These two go hand in hand. If you change one, you change the other. If you change both, you can totally change how you view reality and this can lead to profound change in your actual personal reality. I'm not just talking about you feeling better. This isn't just restricted to your thoughts and emotions. Your actual waking reality changes for the better. You can become more effective and you might appear more positive to people around you.

HOW DOES THIS PLAY OUT?

Start with the realization that you're always judging the stimuli that you get from the outside world. This judgment forms thoughts. This process is never neutral. It always comes from somewhere.

By the same token, your thoughts are never foregone conclusions. You are not doomed to conclude one particular way. Just because a set of stimuli usually makes you feel sad, angry, dispossessed, put upon, oppressed, or otherwise lousy in the past, doesn't mean you have to automatically feel that way now. What if I told you that if you gave that same set of facts to another person, that person can walk away with a different conclusion?

How come? There are always two or more ways to interpret facts. Two people can be presented with the same set of information and walk away with completely different emotional states. The difference depends on how they choose to process that the same info. This difference in mindset leads to them coming up with two totally different conclusions. They don't necessarily have to feel depressed. They don't necessarily have to feel sad or hopeless. They don't have to feel negative at all.

You need to understand how this works out because your conclusion, as natural as it may seem to you, is ultimately a choice. You can choose to look at your situation and its facts from a totally different perspective. If you do so, you may be surprised as to how different your conclusions could be.

There has been psychological research done on siblings who grew up in very challenging situations. Maybe they were going through abuse, maybe they were dealing with the trauma of war, or they had to handle serious deprivation. Whatever the case may be, these siblings had essentially the same set of facts. They were getting the same stimuli from the outside world.

However, these studies show that some siblings went on to become happy, well adjusted, and otherwise successful adults. Others led very destructive lives marked by divorce, drug abuse, and other forms of negative behavior. How can this be when both groups dealt with the same set of facts?

It all boils down to how we interpret the facts. It all boils down to judgment. It either works for you or harms you. It's your choice. Ultimately, you have to pick the interpretation or judgment that encourages, motivates, and pushes you forward. At the very least, pick interpretations that harm you less.

THE KEY: AWARENESS

The key to interpreting external stimuli in a self-empowering way is to simply become aware of the fact that you are judging. If you're reading something right now, you are judging the text. If you're thinking about somebody right now, you're judging that mental image or memory. Whatever form it takes, you're always judging. And for you to be a happier person, you have to first be aware that you are involved in this judging process.

This is the first step to turning your life around. It's a crucial step because without awareness of the process, progress is impossible. You have to choose to be aware that you are constantly making judgments.

These judgments or 'hunches' may seem automatic. They may flash quickly in and out of your mind. Regardless, they are still intentional, purposeful, and ultimately, you have a lot of control over them. Choose to be aware that you're constantly judging and you're constantly choosing to notice certain things over others.

THE NEXT STEP? FIGURING OUT HOW

The next step in CBT is to understand how your judgments are made. There's a reason why certain people, when presented with a specific set of facts, always come up with a negative judgment. It seems that no matter what's going right in their lives, if you give them those facts, they come up with a negative judgment. Like clockwork.

By the same token, other people, when given the same set of information, always come up with a positive judgment. What gives?

It all boils down to a concept called "personal narrative." This is where your judgments come from. This is the filter that determines whether you are going to interpret certain things going on in your life in an empowered and positive way. You can also look at these facts as further evidence of your perception of yourself as a small and powerless person living a hopeless life.

Be aware of how your narrative works. Be aware of the fact that you are constantly judging. The key to all this is the narrative that you choose.

Narratives are chosen

They are learned behavior. Just because you are operating from a negative narrative now doesn't necessarily mean you're stuck with it for life.

CHAPTER 4:
JUDGE TO EMPOWER YOURSELF BY WORKING FROM ANOTHER NARRATIVE

If you order two computers from Dell with no operating system, you essentially have two computers that can't do anything.

If you install an operating system on one computer that makes it only do spreadsheets, you have yourself a spreadsheet or business computer. On the other hand, if you have a machine that you install an operating system that only plays games, you have yourself a gaming machine.

If you look at both computers, it's very easy to think that they're two totally different machines because one machine only crunches numbers, while the other plays a tremendous variety of games. One is very big on multimedia and the other offers a pretty much plain vanilla experience.

They're the same type of machine. The only difference is their installed operating system. Their capabilities and activities are vastly different because of the difference in operating system, not any fundamental physical or hardware design difference.

The same applies to people. All of us, on a physical level, are capable of the same range of activities. However, people do tend to act differently from each other. These differences are not small.

Different people do things differently. They live at different places, they drive different cars, they make different amounts of money, they have different sets of friends, and their life outcomes are different in terms of health, and so on and so forth. But if you were to cut through all the differences and strip away all the programming, people are not all that different from each other in terms of hardware or physical capabilities.

What accounts for all these differences from person to person? It all boils down to the operating system we choose to install.

If you're having a tough time dealing with rejection, overcoming anxiety, or you're just riddled with negative thoughts and doubts all the time, please take hope from what I'm about to say. There's nothing fundamentally wrong with you. You just chose the wrong narrative to believe in.

If you were to override or 'reformat' that narrative and install a new one, chances are very good that you would be living a much better life. At the very least, it would be a life that is different from the negative life that you feel condemned to. You don't have to feel 'stuck.'

YOU CAN DO A LOT TO CHANGE THE DIRECTION OF YOUR LIFE

You actually have a bigger role to play in how everything plays out in your life. This is where the power of narratives comes in.

The reason why you're going through a tough time mentally, emotionally, and physically is your choice of narrative. You might also be facing struggles in your career and relationships because of how you view yourself, your life, and your capabilities. You have to be aware of how you choose narratives.

Be aware of the power of narratives. Open your eyes to making better narrative choices. Make a decision narrative to hang on to and which ones to let go.

THE MOST CRIPPLING NARRATIVES

The most crippling narrative that you could ever choose to believe in will fool you into thinking that everything's a judgment of you. That's right, according to this narrative, the world revolves around you. Everything that's going wrong reflects on you. It's all about you!

You feel the weight of the universe on your shoulders because you are the center of your personal universe. You take everything personally. If somebody's not having a good time or somebody says a mean word, it all goes back to you. You experience a cascade of emotions flowing from the following narratives: you're not worthy, there's something wrong with you, you are guilty, you did something wrong, etc.

You may be thinking that this is crazy. You may be thinking that people do not consciously choose to think this way. They do.

The reason why it plays out this way is because most people like to adopt a narrative where they feel entitled to an easy life. They feel entitled to respect. They feel entitled to feeling emotionally good each and every time. Regardless of what they do, regardless of where they are and who they're with, they feel entitled to things being easy on them on a physical, emotional, and financial level.

One common way you can tell if people have an entitlement mentality is when they say, "That's not fair," or "I deserve better." When you strip away all the surface differences and connect the dots, it all boils down to a narrative where you feel that everything is all about you. If something goes wrong, then it's a judgment of you. If you don't feel right about something someone said to you, it's some sort of judgment.

This is a very toxic narrative to hang on to because you feel the weight of the universe on your shoulders. You are the center of your personal universe and you end up engaging in the following behaviors and mental processes.

YOU BLOW THINGS OUT OF PROPORTION

Since everything is about you, if something goes wrong, it's a judgment either against or for you. It's very hard for you to accept that certain things just happen. You feel compelled to blow things out of proportion because it's somehow, some way, a negative judgment of you as a person

EVERYTHING IS A JUDGMENT OF YOU

It doesn't matter how many choices other people have made, when you interpret their situation, you always feel that it reflects badly on you. Alternatively, you feel there could have been something you could have done to avoid the negative situation. Whatever the case may be, you take it upon yourself to be THE prime mover of what's going on in your personal life.

It is not a surprise that people who feel like this also feel powerless. If you think about it, these two situations go hand in hand. How come? Your system can only tolerate so much pressure. If you automatically assume and feel at fault, at least in your mind, for what's going on, it's easy to feel trapped. It's easy to feel powerless. It's easy to feel like your personal world is just spiraling out of your reach.

Everything has become a judgment, and it becomes very easy for you to feel less and less in control.

SELF-CENTERED NARRATIVES ARE TOXIC

Of course, the scenario above I described is an exaggeration. We all entertain varying degrees of self-centeredness, but ultimately, it all boils down to self-absorption. Feeling that everything is either a reflection of you or relates to you on some level or other. The more you hang on to this narrative, the more toxic your emotional state becomes. Why? It's all about you. Thankfully, this isn't true.

The world is an independent place. The world has its own agenda. There are many different people making all sorts of decisions in the world. You don't know these people, but the way you choose to organize your world and think about what's going on, you think it all leads to you. Your self-centeredness leads to you bearing the brunt of what's happening in your world.

Make no mistake about it, you're going to run into people who are not very nice. These are people who are not having a good time. Believe me, most of the time, the reason they feel that way has nothing to do with you. The worst thing that you can think is to believe that it's your job to make them happy or, on the other hand, they are unhappy because they just don't like you.

The world's issues have nothing to do with you. The world spins on its own axis. It has its own agenda. You have to let go of your self-centered narrative. It doesn't have to be about you. In fact, if you think about it, most of the time, it's not about you. There are just certain things happening in people's lives that make them act a certain way.

Just because they act that way doesn't mean that you're a bad person or that you owe them something. Let go of a self-centered or self-absorbed narrative so you can have a more empowered and positive series of responses to whatever the world throws your way.

CHAPTER 5:
TAKE INVENTORY OF YOUR PERSONAL NARRATIVES

Now that you have a clear understanding of how narratives work and how you draw your interpretations and judgments of your thoughts from your narratives, the next step is to take inventory.

You need to understand that everybody has narratives whether you are aware of them or not. What makes this very challenging for a lot of people is because this step forces people to pay close attention to how they think.

Now you may be thinking that this is fairly straightforward, and you might be thinking that this is very easy to do. Well, it's too easy to think that way, but the problem is we are often very emotional regarding how we think. We get territorial. We're very protective of the implications of our narratives.

Not surprisingly, a lot of people would like to believe that they are a totally different type of person. In reality, their narratives, their actions, their thought patterns, and the things they say all indicate that they're a totally very different person from whom they think they are.

Sounds delusional?

Welcome to the club! We all suffer from some level of delusion. We all would like to think that the way we think, talk, and act are aligned with our ideals. We would like to define ourselves on a practical level based on who we think we should be.

Having ideals and role models is great, but if you constantly define yourself in those terms and let those terms cloud your understanding of your true narratives. You're not going to get anywhere. You're simply just going to be living in denial. This is especially true for people who have parents who have high expectations of them.

In many cases, a lot of people live based on the expectations of others. Therefore, their ideals, or at least their self-definition is being set by somebody else. You have to let go of all of that. You need to become clear as to who you really are. This is going to be tricky because whenever you observe anything, you are constantly changing it based on how you interpret and filter it.

What makes this really challenging is you're going to take off all your filters. You're going to call things in your life as they really are. You're not going to describe them in terms of what you think other people would expect. You're not going to focus on what you should do; rather, you should focus on how things really are in your life.

You need to free yourself from the idea that you should define yourself based on how you should be acting. Instead, you should describe what's actually going on as they are. If you're unable to do this, no progress is possible.

CBT only works if you're dealing with real data. In other words, you have to get real. You have to be completely honest. You have to let go of any kind of delusion or denial. Look at yourself and your narratives with eyes wide open.

Don't assume anything. Don't expect anything. Just focus on how you truthfully think, and the narratives that you actually subscribe to.

GIVE YOURSELF TIME

Give yourself about three weeks to study how you respond to the world around you. You'll need this time to do a realistic and honest self-assessment.

If you flip the script and, for example, write down how we choose to describe ourselves, we're probably going to get a bad reading. You're very likely going to get a picture that is completely different from how you really are.

You have to understand that people talk a good game. Even the most dysfunctional persons throughout the world who cause a lot of harm and a lot of unnecessary suffering around them, would probably describe themselves in at least neutral terms. You're not going to get a realistic idea of what's really going on. That's just how the human mind is set up.

It's truly important to look at how people actually behave. Pay attention to how they truthfully respond. Don't look at a self-assessment. Don't look at self-regard. Don't look at any of that.

Self-description can only go so far and sadly, for the most part, it doesn't go far at all. The best approach would be to study how you respond to the world around you.

When somebody says something take note of what was said and write down your honest response. Did it annoy you? Did it make you feel bad? Did it trigger low self-esteem? Did it make you feel like you hate yourself? Did it trigger anxiety in any form? Whatever the case may be, be completely honest about your response to the world.

You should keep a journal where you catalog all the external stimuli that you get and how you respond. It may be too much work to categorize everything at this point, so only write an ongoing honest description of your mental responses.

Limit your entries to just descriptions. Do not analyze yourself. You're not trying to categorize your feelings. You're not trying to second-guess yourself. You're not trying to "get to the bottom of the situation." Don't do any of that. Stick to simple description. This is the key to effectively and productively cataloging your thoughts.

You need to catalog your mental responses. What's also important is to make sure that you're clear as to what caused your response. You have to be able to trace it back to a stimulus or a set of stimuli.

CROSS-REFERENCE WITH WHAT YOU SAY OR HOW YOU RANKED

Once you have cataloged what you think about when certain things happen, the next step is to take things one level further. If you're like most people, once you perceive external stimuli, your reaction is probably not just going to stay in your head. You're bound to say something and maybe even do something. Whatever it may be, cross-reference the stimuli to the mental response to whatever you say or do.

Again, there's no right or wrong answer here.

You should not censor yourself. You should not feel so bad about what you did or said that you leave it out, or you interpret it in a positive way in your journal. These reactions are not going to help you. What's important is that you accurately write down the chain reaction that's going on through your head.

It all starts with what you choose to perceive and pick up from the outside world. It then proceeds to your judgment or interpretation of that stimuli. This then culminates in you saying something or doing something. You need to cross-reference these elements.

CONNECT THE DOTS

After about three weeks, you should already have quite a bit of material to work with. In fact, if you are really serious about doing this, then after one day, you should already have quite a lot of notes.

After three weeks, you need to read through everything you've recorded. Try to connect the dots and look at how these responses are related to each other. When you respond a certain way, chances are there are many stimuli falling under a specific category which triggers a similar response. Look for grand patterns.

What makes this really difficult is that this information is not all going to jump out at you. To succeed with CBT, you need to look patiently through all your behavioral and thought patterns and figure out connections. It's not going to be a simple case of just putting 2 and 2 together. You have to be patient with all the information you get, because it may seem like you're repeating the same things over and over again.

If you see a repeating pattern, get excited. This is good news actually. If you see the same response repeating itself time and again, based on a fairly narrow range of stimuli, this means you are onto something. This means that you are seeing that a particularly limited range of stimuli can reliably produce a certain response from you.

TIE THE PATTERNS TOGETHER

Since you know that there is some sort of internal logic to your responses, you need to come up with some kind of explanation or some kind of logic why such responses take place in the sequence they do. This gets you one step closer to putting together a story.

Keep in mind that narratives are always stories. They may take the form of a one sentence story, but they're still stories. Narratives are very powerful, but their power oftentimes comes from the fact that they are tough to explain. Indeed, it's extremely hard for you to put your finger on them just by thinking about them.

Accordingly, you need to look at your actual responses in this three-week period. By looking at this data, you will be able to connect the dots and see the grand patterns that point to the stories you're constantly playing in your head. This is how you get closer and nearer to accurately describing the narratives in your life.

FACT: EVERYONE IS A COMPILATION OF STORIES

Everybody has a story. We are always playing a script on the back of our heads.

Now people are not going to own up to this. It's not like you can step up to somebody and ask them what kind of story they have about themselves. You'll draw blank stares. Regardless of whether people are aware of it, everybody has a story. That's how the human mind operates.

Your job is to figure out the stories that define you. These are often not verbalized. Most of the time, you are not conscious of them. Still, these different stories and scripts define how you think, the things you say, and your actions. You carry your narratives with you. It's also important to understand that these narratives are situation based. Put simply, there is no one overarching narrative which works for you 24/7.

In many cases, when something happens to you, a narrative comes to the surface. You draw your interpretation of the things happening to you from your narrative. Another situation happens, and another narrative comes up. These vary situation by situation. They form a context.

Keep in mind that there's really no right or wrong ultimately with narratives. What makes them true or false is how we use them. Their truth value also depends on the quality of the reasoning we used when putting them together. Regardless, your narrative acts as of a reality filter. While on an absolute level, there's really no right or wrong narrative, they can have drastically negative effects if used in the wrong context.

There are certain things about you that are unique to you. These traits and narratives make you special and one of a kind. However, you share quite a large number of things in common with most other people. This mixture of unique and common narratives is what makes pulling apart and figuring out your personal narratives so confusing and difficult.

There are just so many different layers that you have to work with. Still, if you have gone through this process and clearly cataloged your mental responses, and you tracked them to your behaviors and identified triggers, you should be able to put together some sort of story that governs a particular situation. That is your narrative for that situation.

WE WRITE OUR STORIES AND BUILD ON THEM UNCONSCIOUSLY

Keep in mind that your narrative is something that you have picked up unconsciously somewhere in the past. It's something that you picked up along the way. The good news is that you picked it up-you weren't born with it or it was imposed on you against your will.

You chose your narratives. It is learned. Just like anything else that you have learned in your life, you can choose to unlearn it. Just like you would install an operating system on a computer to do a specific job, you can always choose to reformat the hard disk of that unit and install a different operating system. Once you do that, the computer will do other tasks.

The same applies to your stories. You may have picked them up unconsciously, but the fact that you hang on to them means, at some level or other, you feel that we're benefiting from them.

At some level or other they explain reality. You feel they produce some sort of benefit. Now that benefit, if you are hanging on to a very negative narrative, might not be all that substantial in the grand scheme of things, but you at least feel that there is some benefit there. So you hang on to it.

You filter all your experiences through these stories. You make facts fit them. They tell you your limits, what you're capable of, certain "truths" about human nature, and, ultimately, your definition of reality. This is important stuff, because as I've mentioned before, two people working with the same basic set of facts can think, speak, and behave very differently. It all boils down to the narratives each individual chooses to subscribe to. We all have this choice.

After recording your personal and mental interpretations of what's happening in your life for three weeks, you should be able to get a fairly clear picture of the different stories you're hanging on to.

CHAPTER 6:
LET GO OF SELF-CENTERED NARRATIVES

Now that you have a rough collection of the stories or personal scripts that you play in your mind constantly, the next step is to let go of some of them.

It should be obvious that not all the narratives that you play consistently in your head do you good. In fact, if you're reading this book, there's a decent chance that a lot of them are harming you or frustrated. Maybe they make you feel small, powerless, or 'stuck.' Perhaps you feel some of your narratives are holding you back from your fullest potential. Whatever the case may be, these personal stories that you use to filter reality are somehow preventing you from living a life of consistent victory.

In this chapter, we're going to let go of the low-hanging fruit as far as your negative or not so optimal narratives are concerned. We're going to let go of the most obviously counterproductive first.

As I mentioned in Chapter 4, there is one type of personal narrative that is absolutely toxic-self-absorption. According to this personal script, the whole world-even the universe-revolves around you, your need for comfort, your desire for convenience, your sense of fairness, and everything else you feel you deserve. Obviously, the world doesn't revolve around you. Accordingly, you have to let go.

Again, spoiler alert: the world is not about you. The world has its own agenda. The world spins on its own axis regardless of your feelings. No matter how hard you wish or try, the world is not going away any time soon. You, on the other hand, have a definite expiration date.

Most human beings do not live beyond the age of 130. That's just the mortal limit that we all have to face sooner rather than later. The world, on the other hand, will probably continue unless we ourselves choose to blow it up.

Understand how this all works. Understand your place in the cosmic order of things. Understand your magnitude and how small you are in light of everything else that is happening.

If you're having a tough time wrapping your mind around this, I want you to play this little mental exercise. I want you to close your eyes and imagine looking at yourself in the room where you're reading this book. See the image> You see somebody 20 feet away from reading this book. Got it? Now zoom out one mile, so that you see yourself in a neighborhood or a city, surrounded by buildings, reading that book. There are a lot of people around you, but you can still see yourself in that building.

Now zoom out a hundred miles. Looking down from the sky, you can see the state or region you're in surrounded by other nearby regions. Zoom out 300 miles and you see the country that you're in, and neighboring countries. Zoom out some more and you see the continent your country is in. Zoom out a hundred thousand miles, and you see the earth. All of it. What a beautiful blue orb floating in the vast blackness that is space. Don't get too attached though... Proceed to zoom out one million miles, and you see the earth revolving around the Sun. Zoom out ten million miles and you see the sun mostly. You barely see the earth.

Do you see my point? If you are to zoom out enough, you see our solar system, and then you see the galaxies, and so forth. I don't mean to make you feel worthless by pointing out how small we all really are. My point is that you need to have the proper perspective. Being tiny and part of a larger cosmic play over which you really have no power over is perfectly okay. It really is. Why? That smallness in the big scheme of things is our shared reality.

You need to zero in on the smallness of your being. You're only here for, in light of Earth's geographic age and history, a blink of an eye. If you look at how long the universe has been around, and consider how long you've been alive, you don't even register. That's how small you are. That's the point in history you occupy.

All this political drama of people getting elected, assassinated, revolutions, wars of religion – you name it-and all the emotional intensity and drama it all brings, ultimately amounts to nothing. We're just a momentary detail in space and time as far as Earth is concerned. And I haven't even started talking about the age of the universe! The verdict? We're only a tiny blip.

Again, I don't mean to destroy your sense of importance, I just need you to develop a humbler, less self-centered perspective because a little humility goes a long way. You don't have to be Atlas. You don't have to be a demi-god holding up the world on your shoulders. You can shrug the world off your shoulders. It's perfectly okay, because that's not your job.

It's not your job to be the center of the universe. It's not your job to be the conscious filter of everything that exists today. That should not be your perspective. Instead, you need to welcome the narrative that you are just a passing entity in this grand play that has gone on for billions of years before you were even born and will go on for a very long time to come. And it's all perfectly okay.

The world is not about you. The world has its own history and trajectory. It is perfectly okay to just let go. You need to let go of that narrative where you are constantly the center of everything. Everything happening in your life doesn't have to be a judgment of you. Everything doesn't have to involve your feelings. Step away from that. Humility-that sense of smallness-is the key that will turn the lock on this toxic mental prison door.

I hope you are enjoying reading! Please share your story by leaving an **Amazon review** Leaving review only takes a few seconds and it will enable me to continue to produce high quality, enriching content to serve people like you.

CHAPTER 7:
THE POWER OF HUMILITY

Let's get one thing clear: among all the different human virtues out there, humility doesn't exactly get top billing. In our modern culture, we tend to focus on virtues that enable us to get what feeling is coming to us. We have this idea of what we deserve and of living life to the fullest. We celebrate taking action. We celebrate confidence. Oftentimes, we celebrate ourselves. The idea of having to wait so you can enjoy your reward later not only seems outdated and old fashioned, but often flies in the face of our modern value system. One of those old-time values that we have kicked to the cub is the concept of humility.

As recently as the 1930s, there were many who championed and idealized, as far as popular culture goes, the values of humility and modesty. It's perfectly okay to believe that you don't know everything. It's perfectly okay to believe that you're neither the center of the universe nor the center of every conversation you're in. In fact, for the longest time, humility and modesty were encouraged in American culture. These were desired.

Fast-forward to today. A lot of people automatically equate being humble with having low self-esteem. Our modern thinking is that for people to succeed, they must first feel good about themselves first. Accordingly, a lot of school systems adopt educational philosophies that prize self-esteem before accomplishment and achievement. Achievement, it is assumed, springs from a healthy bedrock of self-confidence and positive self-esteem. Sadly, this flies in the face of scientific literature.

It turns out that if you want to develop sustainable self-confidence and nurture self-esteem to help push your life forward, you need to build these on a solid foundation of achievement and accomplishment. This means that all those participation trophies and feel-good awards ceremonies where everybody's a winner are misguided. This is just a part of the overall self-centered philosophy that has really pervaded and saturated our mass culture.

We want our rewards now. We want to be the center of the show now. Any value system that involves paying your dues or simply having to wait in line is dismissed as old-fashioned. Indeed, the notion that you have to sacrifice a little bit of yourself for the common good seems downright quaint. This really is too bad because there's a lot of value in the concept of humility.

Humility doesn't have to be a bad word. It doesn't have to mean that if you don't have everything and don't understand everything that you should admit defeat or admit to some sort of defect. It doesn't have to involve some sort of humiliation. Sadly, in the modern mind, humility has been so degraded as a personal value and virtue that it has often been equated with a sense of powerlessness. According to this thinking, the moment you admit or assume a position of humility, you have abdicated your personal power.

THE IRONY OF HUMILITY

The big irony of humility, as far as CBT and personal narratives go, is the fact that it's actually very empowering. I know it sounds crazy. I know it's counter-intuitive, but the fact remains that you grow more powerful as you learn to let go and move on. You have to understand that the flip side of humility is a supreme or abiding confidence in your ability to both get things done and understand what's going on in your life. You and I know that this is often not the case. In fact, if this were the truth, then you probably would not be reading this book in the first place.

You're struggling. You're facing difficulties. There are certain issues that you're trying to confront. Unfortunately, the whole idea that we have to be the center of our identity and relationship with the world becomes a cause of pain. Self-centeredness causes frustration.

If we keep hanging on to the idea that everything going on in our lives is about us, it ends up robbing us of our power to change our situation. If we become overly sensitive, it's very hard for us to separate our perceptions from our emotions. It's very easy for us to think that everything is a judgment about us-either it makes us look good, or it doesn't. It's easy to reduce everything into black and white. We end up blowing things up out of proportion and become too touchy. Any little challenge is often enough to frustrate us.

So what is the solution? What is the truth? The solution is simple: life's not about you. Indeed, if you look at the way the world works, most, if not all of it, is not about you. Furthermore, it's not all that serious. There is a tremendous amount of power that you can unleash within you if you just learn how to let go. Sadly, most people can't.

This is why there is no shortage of whiners and haters on this planet. These are people who complain about everything and everyone. They think that when they're constantly complaining and spinning their wheels about people they don't know and things they can't control, that somehow they remain in control of their lives. The sad reality is that they're not in control. Instead, the more they choose to worry about things they can't change, the more they ignore the things they have actual power over.

The most empowering thing about humility is the fact that when you assume that you are not the center of the universe, you become at peace with that reality. Things start moving in your direction; things start becoming possible again. Why? You put yourself in the position of focusing on what you can control. This works two ways.

First, you have to let go of everything else and focus on what you can control. Now, it may seem like you can't control much of anything. It may seem that your circle of direct control is very narrow and small indeed. However, the more you focus on what you can control right here and right now, the higher the chance you can produce positive results with your actions. Keep producing such positive results and you widen your circle of influence. This is personal mastery. You tend to get good at things that you keep doing repeatedly, especially if you're paying attention and constantly fine-tuning your results. Don't be surprised if you find yourself getting paid more or getting a better reputation. The more you exercise personal mastery, the more your power grows.

Focus on what you can control and let go of everything else. By allowing yourself to feel small for a long enough period of time, you actually end up unleashing the giant that's already within you.

CHAPTER 8:
GIVE YOURSELF THE GIFT OF PERSPECTIVE

Assuming an attitude of humility is one of the most important things you could ever do for yourself. It allows you to enjoy the gift of perspective. If you think in dramatic terms then everything eventually becomes an emergency. Every negative thing happening in your life seems like a crisis. You never run out of drama. You will always operate at peak stress levels.

A lot of people like this mental state, believe it or not. These people would rather feel pain, as long as they're feeling something. In other words, they're so afraid of the numbness or the sense of loss they think they'll feel when they let go. Accordingly, they'd rather live life at a high level of stress and pressure.

Talk about running yourself ragged; talk about living in a toxic mental soup. That's exactly what's happening when you try to hang on to the idea that life is all about you. You think that once you die, the world dies with you because there's nobody left to experience the world. Well let me tell you, the world has its own separate reality. If you die and you're not there to observe, believe me, the world is still going to go on. This is part of absolute reality. Reality doesn't die with you.

You have to let go of your addiction to the self, and the illusion of control that it gives you. Once you allow yourself a healthy dose of humility, you unleash perspective. Things aren't that serious; things aren't that big. Most certainly, things aren't as dramatic as you think they are. The sun will still rise tomorrow. People will move on and get on with their lives. This is one of the most liberating things you could do for yourself. It's a great way of resetting your mental and emotional energy levels so you can become a more effective person.

When you truly believe that you are not the center of the universe, and that there are other competing interests and objectives out there bigger and worthier than you, you will be okay. You won't lose a thing. Well, not quite. You do end up losing the delusion and false sense of security which being self-centered brings to the table. Furthermore, you end up gaining perspective regarding the following.

YOUR PROPER RELATIONSHIP TO OTHERS

When you allow yourself to feel contented being another face in the crowd, you start seeing your proper relations to other people. Instead of people existing to please you or fulfill your needs, you understand that you're part of the giant jazz concerto of life. You're playing your piece while everybody else is playing their segment, and you leave it at that. You no longer feel that everything has to flow through you or everything has to make sense to you. You just groove with the music. It was there before you showed up. It will continue to be there long after you're gone.

Knowing your place in the great scheme of things enables you to accept people for who they are. This works to reduce a lot of the unnecessary drama in your life because once you understand that the world doesn't revolve around you and your sensitivities, you become more tolerant of people. You will be able to stop expecting perfection from others, while expecting them to accept you for who you are. Your relationships (and your attitude towards them) become two-way streets.

PROPER RELATIONSHIP BETWEEN THE PAST, THE PRESENT, AND THE FUTURE

Another great perspective that you get is your personal relationship with your past, present, and future. Unless you have access to a time machine, there's really not much you can do about the past except for one thing: you can change your perception and reading of your past. This is one of the most empowering things you can ever do.

If you can't let go of past hurts and trauma, you are letting your past define you negatively. This can ruin your life because you can't to let go of these past perceived and real injuries. Stop being a prisoner of you past by choosing to view yourself as a historical being. You know there are many things that happened in the past that you could read in a very empowering and positive way to help you feel powerful and in control of the present.

As the old saying goes: those who control the present control the past; those who control the past control the future. This definitely applies to personal narratives. If you take ownership of the fact that you are in control of your thoughts and refuse to blame others or make excuses, you can go a long way in developing a proper mindset regarding your past. Your past doesn't have to be a place of pain, frustration, disappointment, and degradation. It doesn't have to involve mental images or psychological movies of your parents abandoning you, slapping you around, saying hurtful words or otherwise not treating you the way you feel you should have been treated.

You have to understand that even in hell, there are still small pieces of heaven. Even in heaven, there is still a way to imagine yourself in hell. It all depends on your perspective. This is why it's crucial to wrap your mind around the concept of humility and shift your attention from the center to the side. If you're able to define yourself this way, then you can develop a new relationship with your past. Of course, this requires you to take full control of your personhood. If you're able to do that, then you can set a different course for your future. After all, your past provides emotional fuel and inspiration for what you do in the future.

If you define yourself as a winner, a victor, and somebody who makes things happens, then chances are your future will be much brighter. At the very least, it would be much better than if you choose to constantly imagine yourself as a victim or somebody who is just continuously unlucky.

PROPER RELATIONSHIPS BETWEEN YOUR POTENTIAL, YOUR PRESENT CAPABILITIES, AND YOUR PAST ABILITIES

The most damaging thing about hanging on to any self-centered narrative is that it may seem to be an act of confidence on the surface. After all, you have to be confident to think that you are the center of the universe, right? Well, not quite. You may be occupying the center because you're trying to hang on for dear life. What you really feel is that you're at the bottom end or at the bottom of the barrel. You don't feel you're all that desirable. You keep hanging on to the center of your consciousness and trying to filter everything based on your needs and what you feel you deserve. The more you do that, the more depressed, discouraged, frustrated, or disappointed you become.

When you adopt an attitude of humility, you understand that your past abilities are just starting points-that's all they are. They don't define you. They don't limit how far you will go. They show where you started. Your past merely indicates what you have to work with. Your past experiences are building blocks if you choose to build on them. This is a very crucial change in mindset because your estimation of your potential, present capabilities, and past abilities has a big role to play on how much energy and focus you're going to put into making things happen in your life.

If you're constantly hobbled by your negative perception of your past abilities, it's very easy for you to define yourself by your past failures and shortcomings. Make no mistake about it, all of us have shortcomings and none of us came out of the gate 100% winners. Even Michael Jordan had problems playing high school basketball. There were many times he was disappointed by his performance and was doubtful of his ability to play basketball.

It doesn't matter how many times you failed in the past. You shouldn't define yourself by those setbacks. What you should focus on is the fact that you have started. At least, you put one foot in front of the other, and you tried your hand at something. It's your choice whether you can continue to keep on building. Adopting a certain level of humility helps you get a proper perspective on the relationship between your past abilities, your current capabilities, and your future potential.

CHAPTER 9:
STEP OUT OF YOURSELF TO GET A HOLD OF YOURSELF

Before we go any further, let me quickly recap what cognitive behavioral therapy is about. CBT operates under the premise that maladaptive behaviors stem from badly formed, imprecise, or incorrect thoughts arising from inaccurate or less than optimal personal narratives. In plain English, the negative actions you take and the emotions you feel come from badly formed thoughts that arise from your inaccurate or harmful personal narratives. You simply chose to read your personal reality negatively.

In other words, there's no space here for blame; there's no bad guy. Instead, this negativity you're feeling is really just a mistake. If you can adopt new narratives, you can live a more positive life because you feel more positive and powered, and this enables you to take more positive actions.

As mentioned in the previous two chapters, one key reason why people have maladaptive behaviors which they can't seem to stop is because they are hanging on to negative narratives. By simply shifting your focus from yourself to others, or to the world in general, you can make tremendous progress in changing your behavior and emotional states. You increase the likelihood that you will feel good about yourself and act like a positive person, which then makes you feel even better, and you repeat the process over and over again.

Instead of this process dragging you into a downward spiral, you can actually reverse the direction of the spiral. If you become more positive, you feel more empowered. This leads you into becoming more competent and having a greater and more positive impact, not only on the people immediately surrounding you, but the world in general.

It's easy to say this; it's easy to say that you just need to swap out narratives and all these amazing positive things will happen. As you probably already know, there are many things in life that are easier said than done; CBT is definitely one of those. So if you're having a tough time letting go of yourself, choose to care about others. If you really want to turbo charge the power of humility in your life, do this one thing: choose to care about others.

I'm not talking about thinking about them. I'm not talking about reducing them into some sort of icon or ritual, where you feel like you're going to feel better if you ritually think of other people. I'm talking about actually caring for others. This is where compassion comes in. If you look at caring for others as another to-do list item or something you can reduce to some sort of ritual, then you're not going to fully benefit from the power of shifting your narrative from yourself to something else.

THE ESSENCE OF COMPASSION

Compassion is the antidote to self-seeking, self-centered, and self-absorbed narratives. If you truly want to gain perspective and experience humility, then practice compassion. Compassion is one of those words so often used and misused that we're in danger of losing sight of its true meaning. The essence of compassion is your ability to feel someone else's pain. You're able to actually step into their shoes and see the situation from their perspective and feel their pain. Why is this helpful?

First of all, when you practice real compassion, things are no longer about you. It's no longer about you helping others to make yourself feel good. It has nothing to do with you. Instead, you're stepping into their world and feeling their pain; it's all about them. Your role is that of a peripheral player helping the person in the middle or the center of your attention to overcome their struggles. Do you see the shift? Do you see the change in priority? Do you see the changed mental and emotional landscape which compassion brings to the table?

WARNING: IT'S NOT ABOUT HOW YOU FEEL

One of the most common mistakes people commit when using compassion to change their personal narrative is that they make it a fully emotional experience. Compassion has nothing to do with you feeling certain things about yourself. It has everything to do with you feeling somebody else's emotions. This is due to the fact that you have taken the proactive step of stepping outside your concerns and trying to see the situation from their perspective. If you're unable to do this, all you're doing is helping other people so you will feel better about yourself. You won't be making much progress because you end up turning altruism, which is supposed to be a selfless activity, into another form of self-seeking or self-serving.

You have to know the difference. You have to be able to make the break; otherwise, you'll fail. You'll basically just end up helping people because it somehow helps you. Your primary objective isn't them-it's you. You'll be back to square one. You'll also tend to help people whom you know will somehow be able to repay the favor. The only way to know that you're really practicing compassion is when you choose to help people who have no way of helping you in return. When there is no payback, you know that you are boldly stepping into a selfless place. Allow yourself to step out of yourself. By letting go of yourself, you give yourself the gift of perspective. You also enable yourself to get a hold of yourself.

Feeling Someone Else's Pain

One critical component of compassion is the ability to feel someone else's pain. This is very hard to do for most people because, let's face it, we already have enough problems of our own. We already have our own personal traumas or trials. To be able to feel other people's pain, we like neatly drawn lines and pre-set rules. One common example of this is the entertainment that we consume. We feel that we're practicing compassion, at some level or other, or at least feeling it, when we cry. When the hero goes through a tough time, or there is some tear-jerking scene in a movie, we feel the pain; it's real. We allow ourselves to feel good about ourselves because we felt the pain.

When we're doing that, we are just engaged in something that's antiseptic. This type of activity that doesn't really have any risk because we're only engaged in entertainment. It's kind of like taking drugs to feel euphoria. You use the medium to unlock certain chemical signals that are already in your system. We arrange those chemical bonds and get a nice chemical high. It's all synthetic; it's all make-believe.

Feeling someone else's pain, on the other hand, through real compassion, has the risk of loss. Why? Well, many times when you really go out on a limb for people, they don't turn around and say thank you. In fact, many times, they're not even polite about it. Sometimes, they even try to slap you back or do something mean to you. There you are, giving what you can and really going out on a limb for them, and all you get is apathy at best and, at worst, downright hostility. You have to understand what you're doing at that point. Unfortunately, if you feel that this person should be grateful and feel lucky that you're helping them out, you're completely missing the point.

Feeling someone else's pain takes you out of the axis of your own pain and confusion, but it comes at a price. You must be able to take the risk that people might not give you anything in return; that you might get a big fat zero at the end. If you're able to make that transition, then you will be able to truly benefit from the power of compassion. Real compassion empowers you by putting your needs on the back burner in service of somebody else's needs. It also empowers you because it reminds you how much power you actually have.

When you help other people, you're able to make things happen. You may feel small right now. You may feel that whatever you do, it really doesn't mean much. But when you help somebody, it creates change. It doesn't matter whether that person is going to acknowledge it or not. It doesn't even matter whether that person is going to be thankful. What matters is that you actually took action. You changed your normal behavior. It didn't have to happen, but you made it happen. Zero in on that. The fact that it made other people's lives better (no matter how seemingly small the change may be) is good. Zero in on the fact that you were able to step out of the crushing gravity of your self-absorption, self-regard, sense of entitlement, and comfort zone to make that happen.

THE REAL NATURE OF COMPASSIONATE HELP

If you really want to help in a truly compassionate way, help people based on what will truly help them. The funny thing about human beings is that it's very easy for us to ritualize and make up all sorts of artificial rules regarding our activities. One of them involves charity and compassion. We'd rather give somebody a few dollars because it makes us feel good. You help somebody who is down – but are you really helping them? When you see that person again and again the next day, did your two dollars really help? How about your twenty dollars? Or your two hundred dollars?

If you see a friend who is constantly in trouble, did your initial help really help them? Unfortunately, we like to compartmentalize the way we help people. As long as we have given that token of compassion, that's good enough for us. On the other side of the equation, there's also the fact that we often impose our will. We help others based on how we feel they should be helped. In other words, we override the actual needs of the person.

If you come across somebody who's homeless, for example, the main thing that they probably need is drug counseling, mental health assistance, or help with their alcoholism. However, it's so much more convenient to just give the person a $20 bill. You end up imposing your will on their situation and, of course, you feel good about it because you're the hero of the narrative; you're the compassionate one.

In reality, you're not really helping them based on the true help they need. Perhaps it may take too much effort or it may seem like a hassle. Alternatively, you may think helping them would require a long journey of recovery with them-and you don't really have that much time to invest on them. Whatever the case may be, this is reality. Whatever the case may be, you end up imposing your will on your efforts in practicing compassion. Ultimately, it quickly degenerates into helping yourself through them. You project yourself to them.

For example, somebody's homeless and you keep saying: "Well, I've been cold like you," or "I've been broke like you. I've been (fill in the blank) like you." In other words, you are looking at the whole exchange in a very self-serving and self-seeking way. You're not leaving any space in the picture for them. You might as well have a conversation with yourself because your face, your needs, or your past is superimposed on them, insofar as you are handling the situation.

Do you see the lack of real compassion here? Do you see the self-deception here? You're not really practicing compassion, but it feels like a workable simulation, or it feels like something that's close enough to real compassion.

HOW DO YOU KNOW THAT YOU'RE REALLY STEPPING OUT OF YOURSELF?

One way you would know is when you keep helping until it hurts. You crack the bonds of selfishness and self-seeking by helping somebody until it becomes inconvenient for you. Make no mistake about it, most Americans can spare twenty dollars, or even a hundred dollars. However, once it reaches a certain point, it becomes really inconvenient. In fact, it becomes downright uncomfortable. That's where real compassion takes place because if you are not inconvenienced, or you feel that you're not really losing anything, you're not really stepping out of yourself. You're just giving some of your surplus. There's still a lot of padding or insulation between your heart and the heart of the person that you are helping. You're not exactly helping on a heart to heart basis.

A more efficient way of helping until it hurts is to simply give your time. Make no mistake about it, your time is your most important asset. Whatever you devote your time to tends to improve, get bigger, or go up in value. For example, if you devote time into working out and put in the time at the gym to build a better body, you're going to look better. You're going to be healthier, and you're going to feel better about yourself. If you invest time in your mind by reading a lot of books and going to seminars, you become a more knowledgeable person. Take it to a high enough level and people will pay good money for your expertise. The same applies to relationships. Invest time in your relationships and they become more rewarding and fulfilling for everyone involved. Time is that important.

PICK THE RIGHT PEOPLE TO HELP

Now comes the hard part, if you thought using the CBT approach to shift your personal narrative through compassion was easy from the previous sections, think again. This is where the rubber meets the road. You have to pick the right people to help. It's easy to love people who are already lovable. It's easy to help people that you know will turn back, shake your hand, and beam a bright smile at your face. It's very easy to feel a lot of affinity for somebody who will shed tears of gratitude.

Unfortunately, if you want to use compassion to change your

personal narrative, you can't pick those people. You have to pick people who are not very pleasant and can't help you back. You have absolutely no connection to them. They have to be so different from you that you can't identify with them in any way. There's no way you can benefit, either now or in the remote future, from your help to them. Also, there's a good chance that they might even be hostile to you. They don't know the extent of your help to them. They might ridicule you. They might even laugh at you. Maybe they'd mockingly point fingers at you, and you would have to take it, and take it, and take it.

This brings me to the final point; it has to be direct contact. You can't do this through a computer screen. You can't do it through an anonymous, faceless third-party organization. You have to be there; you have to roll up your sleeves and actually help these people. If you adopt this level of compassion, you blow away the callous and seemingly permanent focus of your personal narratives on self-seeking, self-absorption, and self-regard.

CHAPTER 10:
PROGRAM YOUR NARRATIVES WITH AFFIRMATIONS

What if I told you that every time you say something to yourself, whether in passing or consciously, you're actually reprogramming your narratives? For a lot of people, this is a surprise because, let's face it, in the course of a day, we tend to say a lot of things to ourselves. In fact, when people stub their toe, it's not uncommon for them to say, "I'm an idiot" or "I'm so clumsy." They often have certain things that they say automatically like, "Oh, that was stupid of me," or "I'm a dumbass." If you're anything like the typical person, you have this habit.

What if I told you that the more you repeat these statements, the more you program the reality that they bring to the table? These statements are not value neutral. They actually say a lot about you. They establish your limitations. They describe your abilities and if you are not careful regarding these statements, you can program yourself to perform way below your potential. One of the most common examples of this is when people are presented with business opportunities, and they automatically say to themselves, "I don't have the money," or "I can't afford it."

Be very careful regarding statements that you keep repeating because, in the back of your head, you may be thinking that you don't mean anything by it. At some level or other, emotionally, you may be thinking that it is just a harmless statement. However, keep in mind that your mind is always picking up the signals you are sending out to the universe. Your mind is actively receiving these. Accordingly, it's not uncommon for people to program themselves to do things that are the complete opposite of what they're consciously trying to accomplish. In other words, they end up sabotaging or undermining themselves.

If you are facing any kind of frustration, chances are this is already happening to you. You have to be very clear about what things you choose to think either silently or out loud. You have to arrest yourself when it comes to negative statements, because these have far-ranging and deep effects in how capable you choose to believe yourself to be. When you say, "I'm an idiot," you program yourself to perform with narrower limits. It becomes very easy for you just to dismiss certain possibilities in your life because, at some level or other, you feel you're not capable. This can all be traced to repeating habitually negative statements.

This negative self-talk feed into unproductive or outright negative narratives you may have. They may even feed into and strengthen narratives you're not all that aware of. Whatever the case may be, don't give fuel to those narratives because they can and will hold you back and drag you down.

If you want to make headway with your narratives, start with affirmations. These are the complete opposite of the sporadic yet habitual statements that you make to yourself. Those habitual statements are often triggered by certain circumstances or events. Absent those events, you don't say them. They are purely reactive. With affirmations, you don't really wait for certain things to happen. You choose to make a habit of saying affirmations and, just like those "instinctive" or "automatic" statements, these conscious affirmations can and do play an effective role in shaping and ultimately reprogramming your narratives.

YOU ARE ALREADY PRACTICING AFFIRMATIONS … JUST NOT VERY EFFECTIVELY

To recap what I just said above, you're already practicing affirmation. The problem is these usually aren't all that effective because, in many cases, the statements that you say are not positive enough or lack focus. Still, they can operate in the same vein as affirmations-they can inform and empower subconscious processes that play out in your conscious life.

To affirmations more effectively, you just need to become conscious of what you're doing when you say certain things. By simply choosing to be aware, you become more receptive to the messages that these statements bring. Make no mistake about it, statements are never value neutral. They always contain some sort of payload.

Be very clear and purposeful regarding the messages you say to yourself. You have to have a plan. You have to have a clear idea as to why you're saying something, how it's supposed to work, and what external changes in your behavior and your speech patterns reflect success with the affirmation.

WORDS MATTER

You are constantly programming or reprogramming yourself. If you're having a tough time controlling the seemingly random things happening in your life, you need to start by reprogramming your narratives with affirmations. Your narratives don't have to lead to "automatic" emotional statements or actions. You're constantly in the equation. You can always change the course of things. You have a lot more control over your life than you give yourself credit for.

This all boils down to simply choosing to become more mindful of the things you say to yourself. Again, these statements don't have to be vocalized. You don't necessarily have to open your mouth and hear words come out. You can just think certain phrases repeatedly. These are also affirmations.

Override Your Mental Operating System With Affirmations

As you probably already know after taking inventory of your narratives, it's very easy to get stuck in certain 'autopilot' thinking patterns. A specific emotion comes over you, and you just start thinking about particular things, and either you become really negative or this produces some sort of behavior that you come to regret later. It's one thing to realize mentally that we are all on this automatic emotional and mental roller coaster; it's another to proactively do something about it.

You can override your mental operating system by simply doing affirmations. At first, they may seem automatic, rote, or even mechanical, but keep in mind that throughout the whole process, your mind is always picking up signals. Your mind is constantly listening. In the beginning, it might seem like you're just going through the motions. In fact, it might even seem downright ridiculous to you. Yet, the more you say these affirmations and, more importantly, the more you allow yourself to listen to them, the more profound their impact will be.

HOW AFFIRMATIONS WORK

Affirmations are conscious statements which you say to yourself that are not just simple generic words. They actually challenge you to take action. They often involve self-definition. By calling to your attention how you define yourself, you create a range of possible actions you can take. Since they are definitional in nature at many different levels, they impact your judgment of your thoughts and the actions these produce. Affirmations also play a big role in the range of emotions you have when certain external circumstances appear.

For example, if you adopt an affirmation that you are the best manager your company ever hired, you will feel competent. You will feel that whatever situation you find yourself in which require managerial discretion and decision-making, your judgment will likely be correct. You start projecting out an air of confidence. This can definitely affect the person interviewing you. Interviewers are looking somebody who has more than "by the book" knowledge of management. They need to sense that you have the inspiration and confidence which can drive their organization forward. You will be able to give the interviewer this impression. How? Your affirmations trigger a sense of confidence people near you can detect.

Turbocharge the Power of Affirmations

You have probably read many other self-improvement and self-help books that involve affirmations. You are most likely familiar with saying certain empowering statements about yourself. You have probably even read books that walk you through the power of definitional statements to help you become a more powerful and in-control individual in your mind. That's all well and good, but there's still a roadblock in front of you.

You're still thinking that this is great on an intellectual basis. Sadly, unless you develop a sense of urgency using these affirmations, nothing is going to change. You need a sense of urgency to take the right actions at the right times. Doing so will have a profound impact on your overall performance. Put simply, you need to turbocharge the power of affirmations.

The best way to do this is to pair the affirmations you say to yourself with certain emotional states. When saying to yourself, "I can do this job because I'm a winner," don't simply go through the motions. Don't just read the statement and go on to the next statement of the affirmation.

Instead, imagine the emotional state of somebody who has done the job, who has learned what one needs to learn, or who has overcome all sorts of adversities. Get into the emotional state of somebody who wakes up daily and performs day after day. In other words, get into the mindset of a tried, proven, and constant winner.

They have a distinct emotional state. Everything is easy. Everything is predictable. Everything is easy to define. There are no free-floating sources of anxiety that can trigger disaster. Instead, everything is laid out smoothly and easily.

You need to allow yourself to believe that things can be this simple and, accordingly, your emotional states can also be as simple. When you pair affirmations with these clearly defined emotional states, you develop a sense of urgency. You are able to milk as much power and raw energy from the otherwise simple words you are repeating to yourself. Keep this up for a long enough period of time, and you start pairing affirmations with specific actions.

The moment you start taking action is the moment your world begins to change.

You have to understand that the world doesn't care about the things you intend to do. It generally doesn't care about your motives. In fact, in most cases, it couldn't care less about the things that are going on inside your head, because that's all subjective. Anybody can say that they intend the best things. Anybody can say that they tried hard enough, at least in their heads. However, none of that matters unless it's translated into actions that the world recognizes.

If you turbocharge your affirmations so that they increase your likelihood of producing actions day after day, you start changing your personal world for the better. The best part to all of this is that it only takes one pairing of an affirmation to action, for you to catch an upward "ride" to better and better results. How does this work out?

When you tell yourself that you are a winner, or that you are the best at what you do, this creates a positive emotional state. This emotional rush may push you to perform at a very high level. Once you deliver excellent work quality or turn in an outstanding performance, you get feedback from the world. You are either validated, or you are shown that whatever you did has room for improvement. When you get positive feedback, you then feel validated, and you feel much better about yourself, and this adds substance and evidence to your affirmations, and you feel even bolder. Since you're in a better emotional state, and you are more likely take even more action. This positive feedback loop can repeat itself over and over. You increasingly become better at what you do while feeling less and less stress.

Have you ever noticed that people who are at the top of their game tend to be cool, calm, and collected when making certain decisions or taking particular actions? Compare their state of mind to people who are just starting out. People who are just starting out are nervous, they're scared, and they don't know what will happen. Accordingly, people who are top performers tend to perform better with less friction and fewer mental and emotional resources required. They might actually know less information than people who are just starting out, but none of that really matters because the low confidence level of the novice or newbie tends to get the better of them.

I hope you can see the connection here between affirmations which you voluntarily trigger by speaking them out or thinking them, and your emotions and actions. Keep repeating this process to produce a positive feedback loop which makes it easier and easier for you to perform at peak levels. Eventually, it all becomes second nature to you. You no longer freak out. You're no longer intimidated. Even if you're faced with a new set of circumstances, you can rest easy in the fact that you've done something similar before and came out a winner. This has a tremendously positive impact on your likelihood of success with the task in front of you.

CHAPTER 11:
BREAK TOXIC CONNECTIONS

There are two parts to CBT. First, there is the prospective part. This involves proactively taking inventory of your narratives and rewiring them so they trigger positive reactions and decisions instead of negative ones. I've explored that aspect of CBT in the previous chapters. For this chapter, we're going to look at the other end of the CBT equation. We're going to look at how certain situations trigger you to think in a negative way. There are particular stimuli that you pick up from the outside world that you feel you can't resist. Once you detect these, you almost automatically feel negative. These are triggers. These can be people, memories, situations, and ideas. Whatever the case may be, they tend to almost always get the better of you.

The reason why they seem so automatic in triggering all sorts of negative emotional responses is because you've made a habit of responding to them that way. You constantly pick out the worst interpretation. If you think about it, this makes a lot of sense on an abstract level because just as with any system, we're always looking to make the easiest, most efficient connections. In other words, we're constantly looking for the path of least resistance. Accordingly, our minds will always look at certain triggers and make the quickest connection because it takes too much effort to thoroughly examine things based on the actual facts

While this "efficient thinking" works out in many different settings-making routine decisions, for example-when it comes to your mental associations, this can lead to a sense of powerlessness. It's very easy to feel that as long as certain situations pop up, your mind and emotions automatically go on autopilot, and you end up doing negative things. It's easy to conclude that there's really not much you can do to break out of this cycle.

For example, it's one thing to say to yourself that you forgive your ex-girlfriend for breaking your heart, but the next time you see a friend of yours tag her name on Facebook, you get triggered. The tears come; the anger flashes. Whatever the case may be, the emotions are strong, and you are probably kicking yourself for feeling that way, but this highlights the fact that there are some emotional habits you need to let go of.

YOU NEED TO BREAK TOXIC CONNECTIONS ON A SEPARATE TRACK WITH NARRATIVE REFORM

Narrative reform, complete with inventory and disruption processes, is important. However, you have to do that separately. It can take quite a while. For you to start feeling better in the here and now, as far as your automatic behavior and thinking patterns are concerned, you need to take steps now in breaking whatever toxic connections you suffer from.

PREPARE FOR SITUATIONS

How exactly do you get off an emotional roller coaster when certain situations trigger a wave of negative emotions that could lead to you making bad choices? Just like with swimming at the beach and dealing with waves, you can just randomly swim around and hope that a wave doesn't hit you, or you can prepare for the coming waves. I hope it's very obvious to you which is the smarter direction to take. It's much better to prepare for situations that trigger you than simply resolving to "steel" yourself the next time it happens.

Usually, when you intellectually think that you've broken apart your habits, and you know the right way to respond, things will still fall apart once you're actually there. It's one thing to talk theory; it's another to actually live through an experience that involves all sorts of real world triggers. This is why preparing for such stressful situations makes a lot more sense. Here's how you do it.

DRESS REHEARSAL

Remember the last time you got triggered? Maybe somebody looked at you the wrong way. Or somebody said a word that made you feel bad? Whatever the case may be, repeat that scene in your head. List down the words, the looks that they gave you, and the wide range of signals that you perceived in a negative way. Once you have that list of triggers, rehearse in your mind how you would respond. There are several ways you can deal with such triggers.

One, you can choose to reinterpret them. Maybe the person was just having a tough time, and had that look on his or her face. Perhaps there was some sort of mix-up you weren't fully aware of, and that's why they were acting a certain way. In other words, it's all on them. It has nothing to do with you. When you choose to respond to a trigger that way, it's hard for you to find yourself in a negative emotional place because it's not about you. This is a very powerful way of taking yourself out of the equation because the issue behind the signal remains entirely with the person sending that signal.

A great approach to this dress rehearsal is simply to go over the different coping mechanisms and approaches you could take to put the judgment on the other person. It's just a miscommunication on their part. They're having a tough time. Maybe they have issues. Maybe they are confused. Whatever it is, it has nothing to do with you. You have to go through that mental list. Furthermore, you have to learn how to take certain factual details of what's happening around you and reinterpret them in such a way that leads to those conclusions.

Another approach you could take to avoid being triggered is to interpret this stressful situation as an opportunity to become a better person. For example, if somebody at work constantly says in group meetings that your ideas aren't very good, you can use that situation as an opportunity for you to become a better person by asking for collaborative opportunities. You could use it as an opportunity to put yourself and your hurt pride aside and reach out and ask that person, "Do you have a better idea? What can you share regarding my performance that would help me do better in the future? Can you help me?"

In other words, instead of instinctively balling up your fist and smacking that person in the head, you open your palm, and you reach out in collaboration. You choose to sidestep your normal reactions to something more proactive, collaborative, and it all might possibly lead to a more positive ending. There are many ways you can do this. What's important is that you go through dress rehearsals. Don't just focus on the words being said. Focus on the visuals. Imagine yourself in a situation where this person says something or does something to you.

Keep going through these dress rehearsals so when they do happen, you're not left with your basic default response. You're no longer restricted to simply reacting to what happens. Instead, you are responding based on your highest values. This is crucial because if you do not respond based on your highest values, you don't develop them. When you don't develop them, you don't incorporate them into your character, and you do a lousy job of communicating to other people around you that you do have those high values.

The bottom line is simple: act to produce positive feedback. At the very least, act so you produce neutral feedback. Believe me, this is so much better than the negative feedback loop your automatic reactions routinely produce.

PREPARE YOUR HAPPY PLACE

Everybody has a happy place. This is not necessarily a geographic place or a location on a map. It can be a happy memory. Think back to when you were kid, and your mom cradled you and lovingly smiled at you. You felt totally accepted, completely protected, and loved. Imagine a scene where you had both of your parents giving you all the attention, love, and care you could ever need.

This is a very powerful memory because you feel complete. There's nothing missing. There's no judgment. When you remember these scenes, you feel there's nothing wrong with you. There's nothing for you to prove. Everything is where it should be. You feel at ease. You need to zero in on such memories and pay attention to the range of emotions they bring to the table. Most people have at least one happy memory. Call this your happy place.

When selecting a happy memory, make sure that you focus on the following: You must feel completely accepted. It must give you a sense of total fulfillment. There is nothing missing in the scenario. There's nothing that you have to prove. You don't have to be somebody you're not. You don't have to impress people. You just are.

You need to zero in on that memory. Once you've done that, write down in your journal the details of that memory. What are the visuals? What do you hear? What do you smell? What tactile signals do you feel? After you have remembered as much of this information, create a three-dimensional picture in your mind of how it feels, looks, smells, tastes, and sounds to be in that happy place.

Once you have zeroed in on that, and you're clear as to the emotional payload of the happy place, the next step is to come up with a very easy emotional mnemonic to call that happy place into mind. In other words, you must be able to call it to your mind at will. What you're trying to do here is to set up a situation where, when you are triggered to respond in a very negative or less-than-optimal way, you can cope by calling into your mind your happy place.

This comes really handy when you're in a stressful situation. This is useful when you are around people who normally trigger you. Instead of just simply resigning yourself to yet another wild and bumpy ride on that emotional roller coaster, you make it stop. How? You apply the brakes by simply calling or triggering your happy place. Just as you are stirred up by "negative stimuli," you can also counteract those triggers with your happy place.

Allow yourself to feel emotionally transported and relaxed. At the very least, when you think about your happy place, things aren't in crisis mode. You're not in a worst-case scenario. You have room to breathe. You have room to connect the dots and understand that there is a way out of the problem instead of constantly getting your "fight or flight" processes triggered.

ADOPT PHYSICAL TRIGGERS FOR YOUR HAPPY PLACE

It's easy to think that your happy place ultimately has to just be a mental response. On paper, that sounds great. On paper, everybody is capable of a mental response to triggers. However, when you are being flooded by all these negative emotions, you really can't reach back easily and find that happy spot and take refuge there. In many cases, it's too little too late. The better approach would be to adopt some sort of physical trigger.

One common way of triggering your happy place is to simply breathe deeply. When you breathe deeply and you measure your breaths and close your eyes, it's easier for you to visualize that happy place. It's easier for you to benefit from the emotional relaxation and sense of completion, contentment, and serenity it brings to the table. There has to be some sort of physical trigger; otherwise, it's too easy just to bounce from one emotional signal to the other and find yourself lost.

You also have to create a positive feedback loop using your happy place. For example, if you are caught in an argument and somebody is close to cursing you out, you need to pull that happy place with a deep breath and then create a positive feedback loop by serenely smiling at them and then talking a bit slower to go calmly through the issues. This puts them at ease. At least they're not feeling that you are going to turn and fight them. At least it creates an opening for genuine dialogue. As you call and draw from the internal happy place you have, it becomes easier and easier for you to smile or even joke in what would otherwise be a tense and possibly explosive situation.

CHANGE POSITIVE TRIGGERS

In addition to a happy place and the trigger for that response, you should also look for positive triggers. When you spot these, allow yourself to feel empowered, positive, and happy. Of course, these have to be contextual. They have to make sense in light of what else is going on. You would not want to find yourself in a funeral, for example, and be triggered by somebody smiling serenely at the deceased and allow yourself to feel ecstatic. That would not make any sense. It has to be contextual. Regardless, you need to do this. Find positive triggers in any situation that will allow you to feel empowered, positive, and happy.

THIS IS ALL GOOD AND EVERYTHING, BUT ... NOW COMES THE HARD PART

All the information that I shared with you in the previous sections is great and everything, but let me tell you it's not going to happen overnight. We're all creatures of habit. As I mentioned earlier, we almost always instinctively take the path of least resistance. That's just how we're wired.

Accordingly, you have to keep at it. You have to prepare your happy place. You have to defuse these negative signals in your head. You have to take the initiative. This takes a lot of energy.

However, the good news is that the more you do it, the more you get used to it. It becomes harder and harder for you to just simply react. Instead, you give yourself the opportunity to respond based on your best values. You're able to put on your best face. You're able to bring out the best in you in what would otherwise be a very negative situation.

CHAPTER 12:
USE THE POWER OF LOGIC TO AVOID OVERREACTIONS

One key reason why we tend to go on really explosive emotional roller coaster rides is our tendency to overreact. We tend to adopt certain logical explanations that truly don't have any strong connection to reality. If you were to take all the emotional energy out of a room, and just lay down all the facts of what is going on, and examine everything objectively, you would be stumped as to why people were so upset. You would be stumped as to why people were so emotional.

In most cases, that's how things are and, unfortunately, we don't live in a library. We don't live in an emotionally segregated world where we just focus on logical connections. We live in the real world. It is filled with emotions. The real world is filled with reactions and instinctive responses.

In this chapter, I'm going to teach you how to use the power of logic to at least take some of the air out of your emotional roller coaster ride. Again, just like with all the other information outlined in this book, this method takes quite a bit of work. This is not something that is second nature to most people. Still, if you work at it and give it enough time to develop as a personal skill, you will get better at it. It will eventually become second nature to you.

THE WORST-CASE SCENARIO ALMOST ALWAYS NEVER PANS OUT

Whenever you're in a heated argument, or you're in a situation where there's a lot of anger or frustration, understand that people often respond that way because they feel they are in a do-or-die situation. They feel that it's really the worst thing that could happen, and they are prepared to fight. They are prepared to do whatever it takes to take care of the issue because the stakes are sky-high. That is the emotional landscape they perceive. However, from a purely logical or objective perspective, this almost always never squares up to reality. Seriously. On an emotional level, personal dramas often seem black and white. But on a logical perspective, the worst-case scenario almost always never pans out.

You have to understand that when you think about the worst thing that could happen, you have to pay attention to what's required for those events to take place. You need to zero in on this logical requirement. If you did, you would notice that a lot of the things that people are so scared about and the people are trying to duck or evade are never even in play. There was no chance of that, but people are acting like it's the end of the world. You see how this works out?

The first step is to have an attitude of disbelief. You just have to take yourself out of the equation and say to yourself, "Prove to me that this is the worst-case scenario." When you ask that question, you're looking for certain components that have to fall into place for you to be emotionally triggered-to the extent that it makes sense in that situation.

BUT WHAT IF THE WORST DID HAPPEN? SO WHAT!

The tip above should be enough to suck the air out of a lot of emotionally corrosive situations because hey, let's face it, for the most part, the worst-case scenario is not here yet. The components are not present – but for the sake of argument, let's assume that they are.

What if this is the worst-case scenario? In this particular situation, you should then adopt the attitude of "so what?" If this is the end of the world or the company is headed for disaster, people are getting killed, you just caught a very horrible disease, or your cancer is stage 4, your attitude should be "so what?"

I know that sounds hard to believe but think about it. Logically speaking, if your doctor told you that you have stage 4 brain cancer, it is too late. Seriously. At best, you'd have a few months to live. What can you do? If you have late stage pancreatic cancer, you are probably looking at a few weeks. Do you think you can buy time? Do you think being outraged, shocked, anxious, or depressed can add more time or value to your life?

You have to adopt the idea of "so what" because the train has already left the station. The worst already happened. What's important is your choice of what to do with whatever time you have left. In the case of financial failure, what are you going to do with the opportunities or remaining resources left available to you? This is a very important attitude to adopt because there are certain times in our lives where we really cannot avoid disasters. They truly are the worst-case scenarios. They really do come to pass. The question is whether we are going to adopt the attitude that will at least enable us to live like victors for whatever time is remaining.

You can always choose to be a victim or a victor. If you choose to be a victim, and the worst did happen, you are choosing to spend the remainder of whatever money you have left or whatever life you have left as somebody who's preparing to lose. It's depressing; it's sad and, ultimately, it doesn't do anybody any good. You're just hosting a pity party.

Conversely, you can look at whatever is remaining and use it as a celebration. Use it as a positive ray of light to highlight a life well lived or identify the victories that did take place in your life. You're going to die soon, but you might as well celebrate the parts of your life that went well. It's your choice because the worst-case scenario has already happened.

THE BOTTOM LINE: IT'S NEVER AS BAD AS YOU THINK

The good news is that the worst-case scenario almost always never happens, okay? However, if it does, then by adopting a "So

What?" attitude, you can get around the crushing depression and caustic anger the worst-case scenario usually brings. On the other hand, always assuming that the worst case has come to pass robs you of your ability to effectively deal with things in the here and now. The situation is never as dire as you would like to imagine it to be. It is never as black or white. It's not a simple question of do or die or victory or death. There's a lot of gray left. In other words, there's still a lot of opportunity left.

USE LOGIC TO GET OVER YOUR FEAR

The underlying emotion in worst-case scenarios is ultimately fear. When we are afraid that this is the worst thing that can happen, fear overtakes us. Fear reduces our options and, ultimately, just leads to worse and worse levels of depression, anger, blame finding-you name it. By understanding that it is never as bad as you think, you're giving yourself some wiggle room. You're giving yourself some space to eventually get out from under the five tons of emotional weight threatening to crush you.

It may seem like a small thing. It may seem like you're not really doing that much to defuse the situation, but a little logic goes a long way. It also grows exponentially. Once you see a crack in the otherwise massive solid block of bad news that you've previously assumed you are doomed to suffer, it's easy to start becoming more and more hopeful. The way to increase the size of that crack is to use logic. Use logic to get over your fear.

Assuming that it's not the worst-case scenario, what exactly is going on? How likely is it that your worst fears will come true? By subjecting this range of connections and mental pictures that you have to the withering analysis of logic, you gain perspective. You buy time. You're giving yourself enough mental and emotional rope to tap the powers of your imagination and creativity to come up with an alternative.

One common conclusion is that you're not really losing much, or whatever you're losing isn't really that big because there is bound to be something offsetting it. By simply using logic just to break down the things you are assuming, you increase the likelihood that you will find opportunities and recognize assets that you may not be aware of. Strengthen your internal logical realizations by focusing on objective facts. This is crucial.

It's easy to confuse emotions with facts. The problem is emotions can play tricks on your mind. Emotions and hunches are often not rooted in reality; facts are. By focusing on what really exists, you increase the likelihood that you will have a more realistic and practical take on what's going on. This prevents you from overreacting because you are basing your response on objective facts and logic.

Again, I'm not claiming that this is easy. I'm not claiming that you can do this overnight. Nevertheless, the more you do it, the better you get at it. Think of logical reasoning for emotional responses along the same lines as working out at the gym. The first time you lift weights, your muscles will probably be very sore for a few days. However, the more you stuck with it, the more you get used to your new routine. Keep at it and you'd be surprised at how much you could lift. The same applies to using logic to avoid overreactions.

CHAPTER 13:
TO TAKE CONTROL, CHOOSE TO BE AWARE

Chapter 12, let's face it, is quite difficult for a lot of people. Thankfully, I have some great news for you in this chapter. Did you know that by simply observing something, you change it? I know that sounds magical, but it's actually backed up by hard science. In physics, this is called the Heisenberg principle. By simply observing a phenomenon, you change the result.

This also applies to what's going on in your head and in your heart. By simply choosing to become aware, you are already starting the process of changing your behavior, the words that come out of your mouth and, most importantly, your emotional, instinctual responses. The best part to all of this is that you're not trying to reprogram consciously. You're not trying to step in there and move things around. You're not purposefully rearranging your mental furniture so to speak. You're not doing any of that. You're just simply allowing yourself to become aware. You're merely choosing to open your eyes to what's going on in your mind, in your heart, and in your logical processes. By observing, you start changing.

OBSERVE WITHOUT JUDGING

Try to observe how certain external triggers bring out specific emotional responses in you. Be aware of the connection. Look at what happens outside of you and trace it to your feelings. Keep focusing on this connection. The key here is to observe without judging. You're not saying to yourself, "This is bad. I shouldn't be doing that." No. You're just looking with curiosity at how certain things bring about particular feelings or specific mental connections. That is the extent of your job at this point in time.

Just observe.

BE YOUR MIND'S MOST AVID STUDENT

By simply allowing ourselves to be merely an objective observer, kind of like a foreign exchange student who just got dropped into your mind to pay attention and log what they witness, you will be able to see many things that you're normally blind to. The reason why you're blind to them is not because they don't exist, or that they're hard to see. Instead, you are so focused on judging them that you essentially deal with the stimuli in an unthinking way. You only need to see, for example, certain elements, and you automatically conclude that they mean something. You just take it from there. You run with it.

It's not much different from a hunter going to the forest and seeing a big tail with a bushy end and a lot of hair in the center. The hunter hears a growl. The hunter then puts all these factors together and starts heading the other direction at full speed. Why? The hunter organized all this information and came up with the judgment that there was a lion several yards ahead of them. If that hunter kept going in that direction, the lion might end up enjoying a two-legged lunch item.

We tend to do this and, generally, it works for us. For the most part, we're able to save a lot of valuable mental processing time by just simply looking at a tiny fraction of a larger phenomenon, assuming that it means something, and making decisions. The problem is if you want to overcome your negative narratives, you have to connect the dots directly. You have to override your habit of jumping to conclusions.

CONNECTING THE DOTS?

Let's just get one thing out of the way. You're already connecting the dots. By and large this is the reason why you're having a tough time. This mental activity is the reason why you're having issues with depression, anxiety, worry, and limiting beliefs which undermine self-esteem and self-confidence. You are doing too much dot connecting.

Now, I'm going to ask you to be aware of how you normally connect the dots and see the gaps there. The reason why you feel that there are certain negative areas in your life is because at some level or other, you're connecting the dots in one specific way. Maybe it's time to reconnect the dots, coming up with new connections and fresh patterns.

Unfortunately, there is no one-size-fits-all formula for this. You have to do it yourself based on your particular set of data. Everybody's triggers are different. Everybody's objective pieces of information are distinct. Still, we all do this. This is one of the few things we all have in common. The difference, however, is that fact that some connections are more productive than others.

You need to look at how you're constantly drawing conclusions from these stimuli based on your narratives. Pay attention to how this choice leads you to act a certain way. After becoming aware that this is going on, start reconnecting the dots. Do you think that you could have a better result if you connected your past experiences and personal narratives with triggers a different way?

SEE THE OVERALL PATTERN OF YOUR LIFE

The reason why automatic behaviors and seemingly self-regulating emotional states seem almost irresistible is because they are set patterns. We feel we can't escape them. However, keep in mind that you are living in a personal prison of which you yourself are the warden. You're the gatekeeper. You have the keys in your hand. The reason why you're staying in that fixed range of options is because you choose to.

Remember, you chose all these narratives at some level or other. It's like living in a prison, and you have the keys in your hand. You see the keys every single day. In fact, you see them so often that they seem like they're not there. But they're still there in your hand. You could always choose to go about doing things differently.

Your narratives, when woven together, form your lifestyle. We all have a distinct lifestyle-a distinct way of living. It is powered by our narratives.

Is the pattern clear yet? Your normal tendency to connect certain dots and leave particular dots unconnected will produce your lifestyle. Your lifestyle then produces your life. Understand how your personal narratives work through this process. Get familiar with how they flow into each other. Finally, understand how they define you.

THE MORE AWARE YOU ARE, THE MORE YOU CAN CHANGE YOURSELF

Like I said, the great news of this chapter is that by simply being aware, you start changing things in your life. The longer you observe how you behave and how you interpret certain segments of reality to mean specific things, the more power you will have over your 'automatic' thoughts and actions. The more you understand which triggers unleash certain emotion states and how these lead to certain actions, the more you can change yourself.

Be aware that this is happening. Become aware that you're connecting certain dots. Be aware that you believe specific patterns are true and this defines your identity.

DON'T TAKE THINGS FOR GRANTED

Now, just as you can be looking at a particular phenomenon out in the natural world, it's easy to take certain things for granted. It's so comfortable to think that once you see exact things then it's easy to conclude specific truths.

On the flip side, if you feel that you don't see certain things, then it is okay not to conclude a certain truth. You should stop thinking in terms of shorthand, and instead choose to look at all the things that are playing out in these patterns with a fresh set of eyes. Allow yourself to question everything. Don't just go by assumption.

Don't take things for granted. Don't be fatalistic and assume that there's really not much you can do about the things going on in your life. Don't be dismissive either. Don't think that just because certain things are there, or they're not there, then they don't really mean that much. Instead, look at everything that is happening and see its value. Try to uncouple each element in your assumptions or disconnect it from whatever it is normally attached to, and try to come up with new connections.

For example, if you are constantly triggered by memories of your father because you did not have a good relationship with him, don't automatically recoil at the memory of certain words or phrases from your father.

For instance, my friend Adam was always told by his dad that he was an idiot. Adam rebelled against his father by smoking a lot of weed when he was a teenager. In college, he ended up, doing a lot of drugs. After graduating, he simply chose to coast through life. He didn't have much drive. He didn't really apply himself.

I lost touch with Adam for several decades. When we finally met up, I discussed with him the revelations I discuss in this book. Intrigued by CBT, he let me walk him through key memories and coping mechanisms he had. I was able to work with Adam to the point where he was able to take the emotional sting out of the memories he had about his father. When he remembers his father calling him an 'idiot' or saying he's 'good for nothing, he now has a different interpretation.

I worked with Adam to re-interpret that memory as his father challenging him to be better than what he was settling for.

Because Adam was one of those "super genius" kids in junior high, he was always easily bored. When a teacher introduced a new concept, Adam figured it out backwards and forwards before the teacher could even fully explain it. That's how quick Adam's mind was. And accordingly, he got really bored easily. And he would always take the easy way out and do as little as possible to challenge himself.

Perhaps his father, when he told Adam, "You're an idiot," was saying that out of love, or out of frustration over the fact that this young person was capable of so much more but constantly contented himself with doing the very least. When we looked at that alternative meaning and we 're-connected' many of his other memories to his personal narratives, Adam's demeanor changed. All that anger and that free-floating frustration that he had with his father started to melt away.

After six months, I met up with Adam again, and he had launched a start-up Internet company that had just been funded a few million dollars. He said to me that our talks about his father had showed him that he could expect greater things from himself. Our conversations changed him, as well as his whole relationship with the concept of ambition and how he defined personal ambition.

It truly blew my mind that Adam had come up with this really amazing idea for a mobile app that is extremely exciting as far as personal productivity and commercial applications go. He had success in him all this time. Still, for the longest time, he chose to interpret his father's statements about him in such a way that it dragged him down, instead of pushing him upward and forward to his fullest potential.

This is what happens when we allow ourselves to avoid being fatalistic and dismissive when we're looking at the dots in our narratives. They may seem like they've been there for a long time. They may seem all too 'natural.' They may even seem logical.

Regardless, there are always other interpretations. Never lose sight of these. Don't be dismissive. Don't think that just because your emotional roller coaster operates one way for so long, you're stuck with it.

CHAPTER 14:
MASTER YOUR EXPECTATIONS

It's very hard to be disappointed if you have the right expectations. In this book, you're probably feeling empowered. You're most likely excited about making some fundamental change to your life. Congrats! That's the way it should be.

I encourage you to look forward to reconnecting the dots that underpin your personal narratives so you can make a better life for yourself. With that said, don't fall into the very common trap of developing unrealistically high expectations.

The problem with high expectations is that you can set yourself up to such an extent that if reality doesn't match the scale and the scope of your expectations, you feel disappointed. This is a very common response. It happens all the time. Do yourself a big favor and be as realistic with your expectations as possible.

Instead of thinking that you're going to turn everything 180 degrees with the information in this book, be more practical. Understand that a 90-degree difference is, for most practical purposes, good enough.

Now I'm not saying that you should lower your standards and constantly aim for "good enough." I'm not saying that at all. What I'm saying is that you should shoot for an initial realistic level of expectation. Otherwise, you might just be making things much harder on yourself. Your journey becomes a lot more difficult than it needs to be.

What are the right expectations you should have? Well first of all, expect to be challenged. Change is never easy. We are all creatures of habit. The number one thing most human beings fear is change. Understand that this is your reality. We're not just talking about other people. This is you. You're afraid of change. You're fearful of the unknown. Understand that and expect to be challenged.

Second, expect to solve problems. The reason why you're feeling anxiety, depression, low self-confidence, and low self-esteem is because you are adapting to the world's stimuli in a less-than-optimal way. In other words, there's a disconnect somewhere between what you perceive and how you respond on many different levels.

This realization can trigger all sorts of familiar negative judgments. You might conclude that there's really no hope. You might even think that maybe you're just a bad person. Stop it. Seriously. Don't go there. Instead, look at this as a giant puzzle. Look at it as you giving yourself the time and opportunity to observe how everything fits, so you can solve the problem eventually. If you adopt a problem solver perspective to any kind of issue, you make it much easier for yourself to eventually figure things out. Feel better? Feel more optimistic and empowered? I told you so!

Compare this to how you normally look at things. You can always choose to view the things that have happened in the past as essentially your destiny. You can conclude that this is just who you are, and there's really nothing you can do about it. This is your destiny in life. This is what you were put on earth for.

Do you see how hopeless the latter mindset is? Do you see how defining the situation in those absolute terms doesn't help? Does it really do you any favors? You have to approach your frustrations and negative mental habits as challenges that you can solve. You have to look at it as a puzzle which you only need to observe in order to overcome it.

Finally, you need to expect to use your imagination and creativity. This is not one of those one-size-fits-all magic bullet books. Let me give you a spoiler. No such book exists. At some level or other, you still have to use your imagination and creativity to appreciate the specific nuances in your life and apply the information presented in this book.

This is how the book will be able to deliver its payload in your life. You have to take the initiative. You have to do the heavy lifting of fitting this information in. This is where your imagination and creativity are involved. You're not just going to be filling in spaces, connecting the dots, or filling out forms. You have to look at what's going on in your life and what's possible. To make that leap you have to use your imagination and creativity.

CHAPTER 15:
CBT BEST PRACTICES

To make cognitive behavioral therapy work optimally for you, you not only need to follow the instructions laid out in this book, but you also need to adopt the following tips:

KEEP A JOURNAL

Keeping a journal enables you to track your progress. After two weeks of implementing the CBT techniques contained in this book, you should have more than what you need to feel good about yourself. At minimum, you should be able to feel great about how far you've come. Even if you are unable to make some big dramatic break from how you normally think, you can still feel good about the fact that you have become more aware. You should have become aware of a lot more information than when you started.

ADOPT A MINDFULNESS PRACTICE

Mindfulness is all the rage in the United States, the United Kingdom, and elsewhere currently. There's a reason for this. While I'm not trying to give it overblown or exaggerated importance, the more mindful you are overall, the easier it will be for you to put into practice the information contained in this book.

There are many mindfulness techniques being sold in a wide range of books out there, and you are more than welcome to explore those techniques. I'd like to direct your attention to three mindfulness practices that I've found personally helpful.

TRANSCENDENTAL MEDITATION

Also known as TM, transcendental meditation simply involves you "reciting" a silent mantra. The mantra is a word that has no meaning. This lack of meaning is the key. Your mantra must have no meaning because the whole point of transcendental meditation is to follow your breathing patterns to such an extent that you pair it with your mantra. You can focus on your mantra to gain a tremendous sense of release, serenity, and peace. When you do this, you center your being, and thoughts become impossible.

You know that you have achieved real internal peace when you can't even form thoughts. That is the end goal of transcendental meditation because that level of mindfulness-the ability to live in the present moment-can pay off tremendously when you are observing your mental and emotional processes and trying to make certain changes. TM's inner calm can definitely help when trying to control your runaway emotional roller coaster.

You can access one of my favorite books on meditation on below URL-

http://geni.us/meditationbook

This is quick and short read which cover everything you need to know in order to start your Meditation practice. This book is specially written for beginners.

SINGLE OBJECT FOCUS

Single object focus enables you to trigger a heightened level of mindfulness by simply focusing your sight on something in front of you. It's that basic. It is so simple, almost anybody can do it.

For example, I wrote this book in between "Grande" cups of Americano coffee at Starbucks. I was looking at one of their corporate social responsibility posters. I saw this poster touting and celebrating Starbucks' support of a local education initiative. To adopt single object focus, I just look at the poster-preferably the center-and describe in my mind what I'm seeing.

At first, I'll probably be listening to the people around me. I very likely will be feeling the cool temperature. However, the longer I look at the object in front of me and the more I try to describe it in three-dimensional terms-what I'm seeing, hearing, tasting, smelling, etc.-the more my thoughts are drawn to the object.

Slowly, a process of displacement occurs. All the sensory input I get from that object starts crowding out the other things that my mind is trying to grasp. I'm unable to judge my thoughts as easily. This is a very powerful technique because it's fairly easy to learn and highly accessible for most people.

The funny thing about single object focus is most people already know how to do it. They're just not aware that they know how to do it.

Have you ever talked to a friend of yours and as you go on and on about something, you notice that your friend's eyes start to glaze over? It's obvious that they're thinking about something else. What probably happened is that they were looking at something, and it triggered an internal mindfulness process. That's the state that you're trying to replicate with single object focus. The big difference, of course, is you're doing it on purpose.

PASSIVE THOUGHT OBSERVATION

One of my favorite pastimes when I was a kid was to round up my buddies, and we would go up to a nearby hill. We would park our bicycles at the base of the hill and walk halfway up this gently rolling hill. We would then lie on our backs and just look up at the nice overcast sky. It would be not too bright nor too gloomy. It was just right. Sure enough, the clouds would roll by, and my friends would have so much fun just describing what the clouds looked like.

The funny thing is that one friend would say a certain cloud looked like an elephant, and another friend would say that it looked like a Volkswagen. There was, of course, no right or wrong answer.

Clouds can look like whatever you want them to look like, and your answer is no better than the person sitting next to you. You're constantly reading your personal meaning on to cloud shapes. You acknowledge the clouds and they move on.

What if I told you that you can adopt the same attitude with your thoughts? This is called Passive Thought Observation. It's a mindfulness practice where you close your eyes and follow your breathing patterns and focus on your thoughts.

However, instead of normal thought processes where you try to grab a hold of your thoughts and judge them and connect them with other things, you consciously do something else. Instead of getting emotionally worked up by your thoughts, choose to just look at your thoughts as they flash in and out of existence in your mind. This activity is similar to being a little kid again, reclining against that hill with your arms folded looking at the clouds. You think one cloud looks like one thing only for the cloud to be replaced by another which looks like something else completely different.

Passive Thought Observation is a very powerful mindfulness practice because it enables you to free yourself and the automatic emotional connection you have with your thoughts. You know you no longer feel like you have to judge. There is no need for you to feel that you have to always be in control. Instead, you give yourself permission to let things go. Ironically enough, when you do this you actually take greater control of your thought processes.

Anybody can adopt Passive Thought Observation. It has a few simple stages; first, you need to count your breath; second, you need to achieve an internal state of peace; third, you have to train your mind's eye to the thoughts forming in your head. Finally, you train yourself to withhold judgment. Just acknowledge the thoughts. No need to analyze or over think things.

There are a lot more steps involved in Passive Thought Observation compared to the Single Object Focus mindfulness or more formal meditation techniques like Transcendental Meditation. Still, the great thing about this particular mindfulness technique is that it gives you the skills you need to efficiently implement all the information outlined in this book.

DON'T RUN AWAY FROM TRYING SITUATIONS

Finally, as you probably already know, there are many stimuli in your life. Some are more welcome than others. If you want CBT to truly work for you, you should not judge the situations and triggers-instead, prepare for them. Instead of cherry-picking the things that you're going to feel good about, or that you're going to handle, just prepare for them.

I've already mentioned how you can do some dress rehearsal in a previous chapter. Please review that chapter so you can see the wide range of preparations and mental and emotional dress rehearsals available to you.

CONCLUSION

CBT has changed countless lives. In fact, CBT/cognitive behavioral therapy is one of the cornerstones of modern psychological care. It's not going anywhere any time soon. It is backed up by a tremendous amount of scientific literature. It works for people.

It doesn't matter where you are located on this planet. As long as you are human and you have a functioning mind, it can and will work for you if you allow it.

With all that said, the problem with CBT is that it obviously doesn't come in a capsule. It's not one of those products you just need to put in your shopping cart, check out at the store, and unwrap at home. It's not one of those things that you only add hot water to, and suddenly it produces a tremendous effect. It doesn't work that way. Instead, you have to implement it.

You have to pay attention to what's going on in your life and how you think. You have to do it step by step. The good news is that the longer you do it, the more results you get. By simply choosing to be aware, you start to get the ball rolling in your journey to a healthier, better adjusted, and more effective you. I wish you nothing but the greatest success.

Cognitive Behavioral Therapy

An Alternative Treatment for Greater Personal Happiness and Contentment

ANIVYA PUBLISHING

BILL ANDREWS

INTRODUCTION

It doesn't take a rocket scientist to figure out that the world can sometimes get to be a bit too much. It's easy to stress out. It's easy to feel like you have the weight of the world on your shoulders. This is especially true if you find yourself around very toxic people. They engage in habitual behaviors or they spout negativity consistently.

Regardless, you find yourself living in some sort of toxic emotional and psychological soup. You're just too stressed out, too anxious and on edge. Interestingly enough, however, you're not technically suffering from chemical-based depression or anxiety disorder. If you think about it, this is actually worse than people living with some sort of mental condition like chemical depression.

"Chemical" depression is a type of depression where your brain's biochemical compounds and neurotransmitters are not properly balanced. Your nerve cells aren't communicating in the most optimal way and you find yourself depressed. In those situations, generally speaking, selective serotonin reuptake inhibitors can help you quite a bit.

Of course, this doesn't apply across the board. There are a certain percentage of people who do not respond at all to that type of treatment. However, for a large percentage of people suffering from chemical or clinical depression, antidepressants and other chemical-based pharmaceutical treatments can help.

Unfortunately, depression and anxiety as well as a generalized sense of unhappiness cannot be simply dismissed as a product of biochemical processes in the human brain. There's a lot involved. You may have two people who have the same tendency for depression, but if their environment and their attitudes are different, there's a high chance that they won't suffer the same problem.

Make no mistake whether you are going through a tough time or a loved one, there is an alternative that you can try. One very effective alternative treatment to depression and anxiety is cognitive behavioral therapy.

This is therapy that involves changing how you look at things. It doesn't involve chemical compounds. It doesn't synthetic materials which you ingest. Instead, it involves you taking control over how you actively look at your world, yourself and your place in the world.

A large number of people report great results due to their use of cognitive behavioral therapy. If you're looking for a solution that doesn't involve you taking a pill and you're looking for a longer term solution than antidepressant or anti-anxiety medication. You are reading the right book.

In this book, I'm going to step you through what cognitive behavioral therapy is, how it works, a bit of its background as well as the components that need to be in place for it work for you. I'm also going to cover step by step directions on how to use cognitive behavioral therapy, and what you should look for if you seek this kind of help from a trained professional.

I'm also going to step you through a bit of the scientific literature that supports cognitive behavioral therapy, the different types of this therapy, its components and the key elements for success. After that, I'm going to give you an overview of the benefits of cognitive behavioral therapy as well as its limitations and criticisms.

Please understand there is no such thing as a perfect therapy or solution for anxiety or depression. There will always be advantages and disadvantages. There will always be room for improvement.

CHAPTER 1:

DEFINING COGNITIVE BEHAVIORAL THERAPY

Cognitive behavioral therapy is not something that you try on yourself. It's just not going to happen. You have to work with a trained therapist or counselor. While you do the heavy lifting as far as your personal beliefs and your responses to the outside world go, you need expert guidance. You need somebody who knows what they're doing and who knows what to instruct you. They must have been around the block a few times so they know what to anticipate.

This is a one common misconception about cognitive behavioral therapy or CBT for short. A lot of people think that if they just read a book on CBT, they would know the ins and outs of this alternative therapy system, and they can pretty much treat themselves.

There's more to recovery through CBT than just buying a book and learning techniques. You have to actually put them to use. This is the difficult part. You have to keep using these techniques no matter how inconvenient they can be. You have to keep practicing them no matter how busy you get.

Given these logistical considerations, it's no surprise that a lot of people think that you need specially trained counselors or psychiatrists to go through a CBT program. Most of the time, the main value these professionals bring to the table is they give you a formal structure for CBT. You can still do it yourself-you just have to give yourself the time, the space, and you need to commit to doing CBT consistently.

It's very hard to get out from under your mental habits if you are trying to do CBT alone. You need to be under the proper guidance of an experienced therapist who not only understands how it works and how its principles can be tweaked to apply your personal situation but who also knows how to measure success.

You have to understand that this is a results-based therapy. You don't just undergo CBT because you're just trying to "feel better". Who knows what that means? It's too subjective.

When you're working with a trained cognitive behavioral therapist, you are made aware of how your interpretations of things happening in your life impact your feelings, your interpretation of reality and, ultimately, your behavior.

The main goal of cognitive behavioral therapy is not just to feel good or feel at peace. Medication can do that. Being with the right people can do that.

Instead, CBT aims for something higher. It seeks to teach you how to effectively interpret life in such a way that you remain positive, empowered and in control. In other words, with the proper guidance, CBT would help you handle your life in a very different way.

People who normally seek cognitive behavioral therapy feel that their life is spiraling out of their control. They feel that they're stuck. It's as if they're watching a movie of their life, and they really can't do anything about it except just sit back and let things happen.

Properly implemented, cognitive behavioral therapy enables you to reclaim your personal power over your life. Believe it or not everything that happens in your life is your responsibility ultimately.

A lot of people try to run away from this truth. In fact, to a lot of people, this is quite inconvenient and uncomfortable.

Unfortunately, regardless of how we feel, the truth is still the truth. We are always in control of how we respond to the world and this response is never neutral. It always has an impact on what we feel and, ultimately, what we do.

Cognitive behavioral therapy focuses on how people make sense of their world in terms of their interpretation. This is the foundation of cognitive behavioral therapy.

When you change the interpretation, you change how people emotionally respond to things, and this can lead to a profound impact on how they do things.

For example, somebody who is suffering from low self-esteem issues usually looks at any situation from a perspective of doubt. They don't think they're good enough. They don't think they're good-looking enough. They don't think people would like them. They don't think they would belong, so on and so forth.

Since this is how they interpret the signals people and situations give them, it is no surprise that they tend to miss out on opportunities or avoid social settings. They doubt themselves so much. They feel that people would not like them. They feel uncomfortable.

This is not just happening in their heads because when somebody has such a low self-esteem, and they're doubting themselves all the time, this can have physical effects .You can physically feel like you're about to throw up. You feel like you're shaking. You want to curl up into a ball or assume the fetal position.

Unfortunately, people with low self-esteem think that this is natural. They've responded to the world this way for so long they think that it's part of them. Some even say it's just who they are. It's port of their personality. No, it's not.

Cognitive behavioral therapy goes to the root of the problem. The root of the problem is not that feel that you're ugly or that you assume that you are going to screw things up the moment you are given any kind of responsibility.

Instead, it goes straight to the issue - your low self-esteem. Why is that? Why do you automatically feel that people are not going to like you? Why do you automatically fear social settings or any kind of opportunity you learn? How are you looking at your situation? Are there any alternative interpretations?

A crucial part of CBT beat is the identification of negative thought patterns. They have to be clear about their thought process.

CBT doesn't assume that there's something wrong with you. Instead, you are first walked through the process of clearly describing how you view yourself, how you interpret reality and how you find yourself in certain situations.

There's no right or wrong answer here. The focus is objective truth. In other words, it's all about accuracy.

The next step is to look at the fought patterns involved and understand that it's just one possible train of thought.

For example, if you go into a bar and you see a very attractive member of the opposite sex turn around, look at you and laugh. If you have a low self-esteem, you would automatically assume that person is laughing at you. Are there alternative interpretations?

A CBT therapist will step you through the alternatives and help you process that memory in such a way that it doesn't lead to negative thoughts and, ultimately, negative actions.

Maybe in that memory there was somebody cracking a joke behind you or making some faces. Perhaps that good-looking person was looking at that person behind you. It doesn't have to be you.

As long as the alternative interpretation are supported by facts, the CBT therapist can help you come up with a healthier approach to processing social information so you get out from under your social phobia.

Speaking of phobias, CBT is quite effective in this field. Take the case of an individual with dental phobia. This person is just deathly afraid of visiting the dentist. We're not just talking about root canal here. We're talking about just regular cleaning.

A CBT practitioner would ask this person about their past experience going to the dentist. The patient would then go through story after story until they get to the traumatic incident that led to an unhealthy association of the dentist with pain. It may have happened when the patient was five years old.

The therapist would then work with the patient to cut that mental connection between dentist and pain. In other words, they help the person realize that what happened in the past can stay in the past. Just because they had a traumatic experience that one time doesn't necessarily mean that all people going to dentists always suffer the same experience. They may just have been unlucky that day.

Oftentimes, the further we are from the memory, the more we blow it out of proportion. We exaggerate. It may turn out that when the patient was a kid, they just experienced slight pain, but as they got older, they remember the pain as something far worse.

An expert cognitive behavioral therapist can help patients go through this process successfully.

CHAPTER 2:

THE HISTORY OF COGNITIVE BEHAVIORAL THERAPY

CBT was formulated about forty years ago to help treat people suffering from depression. As the years went by, a lot of the techniques and steps developed in CBT to handle depression have been applied to a larger set of mental and emotional disorders.

Starting with depression, CBT has gone on to treat borderline personality disorder, bipolar disorder, anger issues, alcohol and drug abuse, childhood depression, spousal or marital conflict, insomnia, eating disorders, fear of the dentist, all sorts of social phobias as well as generalized anxiety. That is a long list, and it's easy to see why cognitive behavioral therapy has expanded quite a bit because there is a tremendous amount of science as well as success stories behind it.

The world of psychology and psychiatry has actually developed on two tracks. There's always been a "talk therapy" component to treating mental, emotional and personality disorders. However, fairly recently, more and more practitioners have been leaning on hardwired or biological treatments involving a range of chemical compounds.

This really all became really popular when the popular antidepressant Prozac entered the global mental health scene. At that point, a lot of people were thinking that depression is just another illness, kind of like the flu. When you have a head cold, you take a pill. When you're depressed, you take a pill.

This has led to a massive explosion in prescriptions for anti-anxiety anti-depression medication. In fact, if you were to study the top ten most-prescribed medications in the United States, antidepressants and anti-anxiety medication will always make the list.

This has raised a lot of alarms because of the fact that these chemicals do have a tremendous impact on the patients' brain chemistry. Without proper supervision and prolonged use, they can have long-term effects on patient's mental functions.

This is why there's been a renewed and intensified interest in more natural approaches to personality, emotional and psychological issues. Cognitive behavioral therapy can work with antidepressant, anti-anxiety and other medications.

However, patients would be better off if they use a completely chemical-free approach. The person often credited as the pioneer of cognitive behavioral therapy is Dr. Aaron T. Beck. Dr. Beck focused most of his research on the study of depression.

In particular, he wanted to see the connection between depression and the cognition or the ability of depressed people to perceive their reality. He noticed that there was quite a bit of a link between depression and people's cognitive thinking.

Prior to Dr. Beck, the common idea was that depression happens and it leads to negative thinking. Dr. Beck reversed the process. He said that if the cognitive state of the individual patient is positive, then depression can be overcome. It can go the other way instead of simply assuming that if a person is depressed, then it leads to negative thinking, and there's really not much people can do about it.

This was a breakthrough because it led to the core premise of cognitive behavioral therapy which involves taking control of how you think. It may seem like your depressed mental state is automatic. It may seem like you really don't have much control over it, but by taking control over your ability to interpret what things mean in your life, this can lead to you arresting that negative emotional slide to sadness, melancholy and, ultimately, depression.

Dr. Erin T. Beck's pioneering work laid the foundation for cognitive behavioral therapy which has then grown by leaps and bounds and is now applied to a lot of dysfunctions and disorders.

CHAPTER 3:

WHAT ARE THE MAIN COMPONENTS NEEDED FOR COGNITIVE BEHAVIORAL THERAPY SUCCESS?

Make no mistake CBT is a viable treatment option for a wide range of psychological, emotional and coping dysfunctions or disorders.

With that said, different therapies have their own requirements. You need to have the right components for any specific type of therapy to work for you.

In the case of CBT, you need trust between the therapist and the patient. This is non-negotiable. Trust is essential to treatment success in CBT.

On the therapist's or counselor's end, that person must be willing to listen to the patient and follow the patient's progress very closely. This requires a deep level of concern for the patient's welfare and a degree of passion for helping others.

Successful CBT therapists must have a strong sense of empathy. They must be open to the specific information shared by their patient. This way, they can configure or adapt the CBT therapy based on the specific set of personal circumstances of the person they're trying to help.

The patient, on the other hand, must be open, sincere and willing to change. This is crucial. If a patient doesn't believe that he or she has any serious problems, it's going to be very hard for CBT to produce positive results. In many cases, it just doesn't happen.

Think of it this way. If you think you don't have a drinking problem, then you probably would not seek the help of an alcohol abuse counselor. Even if you do go, you might not think that the information that person shares with you is going to do you any good. You're not very likely to take up their advice and produce positive change in your life.

Trust, sincerity and willingness to change are crucial to cognitive behavioral therapy's success.

Please understand that even if you are working with the very best CBT therapist, if you're not willing to put in the work and the attention to the change that you're trying to produce, it's not going to work out for you.

You have to understand that at its core, cognitive behavioral therapy simply means working with somebody so you can help yourself. That's really the bottom line because, at the end of the day, it is you who has to change how you look at certain situations, how you read your interactions with people and how you choose to respond.

All of these are controlled by you. Other people can tell you what to do. They can spell out why responding a certain way would produce better results for you but, at the end of the line, you have to make the call. You have to take action. They can't do it for you.

OTHER FACTORS FOR SUCCESS

On top of the patient therapist dynamic, there are other factors involved like the intensity of the sessions. This is very important because when the therapist covers very sensitive territory and the patient intensively studies and focuses on the therapist's guidelines, this can lead to quite a bit of a breakthrough. It also helps if the sessions are not too spaced apart.

Any kind of information being discovered and shared in the sessions must be clear in the mind of the patient. It must be top of mind for that person to learn from that insight and, most importantly, apply it.

If too much time passes between sessions, the patient might forget the important lessons.

It also helps if the delivery of key important concepts is done in a way that appeals to the person being helped. All of us have what their own learning styles.

Some people are very big on ideas. If you're that type of person, you tend to do well in a classroom setting.

Others are more experiential. We'd like to see things as they play out in front of us. This way, we can see the patterns and connect the dots, and this increases the chances that we will put that information into practice.

Others tend to be more social. They'd like to see these concepts play out in a social setting so they can identify them clearly and put them into practice.

These additional factors have a big impact on how individual thinking patterns are structured. It also has a big effect on retraining people as far as their social skills go.

Finally, these factors come into play with CBT sessions that involve problem solving and activating behaviors.

THE BOTTOM LINE: EVERYBODY IS DIFFERENT

I wish I could tell you that you only need to focus on certain factors and you will be okay. Unfortunately, there is no one-size-fits-all or cookie-cutter solution that works for everybody in all circumstances.

Instead, you have to understand these different components. They're like pieces of the puzzle.

Maybe you would perform better if the treatment sessions were more intense. Perhaps you would do better if the therapist puts you in the right setting. It could also be true that you would respond well if the lessons were spaced very closely together.

The problem with all this is there's only one way to find out. You basically have to go through the therapy and see what you and your therapist can change to produce better results.

Right now, before you start going to sessions, all these factors may seem equally important. However, as you try to discover certain things about yourself, how you think and how you learn CBT techniques, you will see certain patterns. You will be able to connect the dots and come up with something that works best for you.

The bottom line is you will only know once you go through it. There's a lot of trial and error here in terms of what would work best for your situation.

What's important to keep in mind is that just because it doesn't seem to work out in the beginning, it doesn't mean that you have to stop. All that means is that you have to trust your therapist fully so you and that person can come up with a solution that works best for you.

EVERYBODY LEARNS IN DIFFERENT WAYS. NO TWO BRAINS ARE LIKE.

You just have to trust your therapist and foster an open line of communication so you can both learn from each other and your therapist can help you realize the right information at the right time to produce the right outcomes.

CHAPTER 4:

HOW COGNITIVE BEHAVIORAL THERAPY WORKS

Cognitive behavioral therapy does not rely on chemicals to change people's behavior. Instead, it focuses on how people view certain memories and certain personal perceptions that they consider the truth.

It may seem pretty basic. In fact, to some people, it may seem like it doesn't really get to the heart of the matter, as far as phobias, depression, anxiety, and other negative emotional and mental states go.

Upon further investigation, it actually goes quite deep. The essence of cognitive behavioral therapy revolves around the fact that the world's stimuli are essentially neutral. Now, this is going to surprise a lot of people.

A lot of people would think that a building that's on fire has to be a disaster. In their minds, there's really no other way to interpret that. Can you imagine a building on fire with orange and yellow bright flames coming out of it, people screaming, commotion, and smoke everywhere?

It's very easy to conclude that there is really a way to look at this situation. What if I told you that two people looking at that same scene can choose to interpret it in two different ways?

One person might think that it's the end of the world. They hear the screams. They fell the heat and they are just paralyzed. They're petrified. They don't know what to do.

Other they run around like a chicken with its head cut off, or they just stare dumbfounded by the tragedy unfolding before their eyes. A lot of people respond this way.

What if I told you that there's another approach? For a great number of people, when they see that same collection of stimuli, they calmly get out of the building, walk to an open space, reach into their bag or into their coat pocket, and whip out a mobile phone.

They calmly call the fire department, as well as the local hospital. They understand that people could lose their lives. They understand what's at stake. They do all of these in a very calm, focused and deliberate way.

Now, let me ask you. Which approach produced better results? Do you think you're helping yourself and those around you if you choose to look at the situation like it's some sort of disaster or Armageddon scenario.

Unfortunately, you're not doing anybody any big favors. If you think that it is the end of the world, you become emotionally paralyzed. You overload yourself with emotions. You aren't good for much of anything. You just freeze up.

Now, on the other hand, if you look at the exact same facts and conclude that this is solvable and that there is a way out of this situation, chances are there will be more people living through that disaster.

There is no dispute as to what happened. The building still went up on flames. People are still homeless. Some people are in danger of burning. The big issue is how to interpret the same set of facts.

The facts are not going to change. What changes is how we choose to respond. This is the core of cognitive behavioral therapy.

You may have had a situation in your life where somebody touched you in a sexual way. This is somebody you trusted. This is somebody who is very close to you. You felt betrayed back then.

You felt let that.

It's as if your world fell apart because this person who you respected, loved, and adored betrayed your trust. Nobody's going to dispute that this actually happened.

The problem is how you're going to choose to interpret that. Are you going to interpret these facts that it continues to hold you back and drag you down from the life fulfilment and peace that you deserve, or are you going to take an alternative path?

Nobody's saying that those facts did not happen. Nobody's saying that you should just forget about those facts because they don't matter. What's important is how you choose to respond in the here and now.

Is your response going to help you lead a more balanced and effectively life? Alternatively, are you going to keep dragging back all these painful memories and making them worse today by possibly exaggerating them, reading in all sorts of frustrations into them, or otherwise playing a trick on yourself.

Unfortunately, a vast majority of people do not understand that they have this power. They do not realize that they have the ability to look at the world in such a way that they don't have to feel sad, let down, depressed, or anxious.

They don't have to be addicts. They don't have to have all sorts of negative personality and emotional or psychological disorders. A lot of those are actually coping mechanisms.

THE CORE OF COGNITIVE BEHAVIORAL THERAPY

Since CBT focuses on changing how you interpret stimuli, it's crucially important that you be clear on how you think. When a person who needs help doesn't think that their thoughts are negative, then it's going to be very hard to help that person.

If they don't think that how they interpret life's stimuli holds them back, it's going to be all that more difficult to get that person's life to change. The core of cognitive behavioral therapy is simple clarity.

Are you clear that these thoughts are negative? Are you clear about the fact that when you think these thoughts and interpret them a certain way, you end up saying the wrong things, feeling the wrong emotions, and doing the wrong actions?

Are you aware that this leads to some sort of vicious cycle or a downward spiral? Let's say you have negative memories in the past.

If you interpret them in such a negative way that you say negative things today, people of course, will respond in such a way that you can easily interpret as negative. You then feel bad and you react in a negative way some more.

It becomes a self-fulfilling prophecy. Who told you that you're ugly? Who told you that you're worthless? Who told you that you're a loser?

Those are interpretations. Clarity is crucial. For a lot of people, clarity also requires trust. You have to trust yourself that you make the right decisions.

Unfortunately, a lot of us have lost trust in ourselves. We feel that our lives are spiralling out of control and there's really not much we can do. Everything is in the hands of other people. We are rocked backwards and forwards by situations outside of our control.

Well, these are just interpretations. We have chosen them. We have control over them. We can take ownership of them if we want to.

The CBT therapist's job is to first get the patient to clearly assess how they think. We're not even going to say that it's negative, positive, or less than optimum. We're not even going to apply any labels to what's going on.

Instead, the therapist just wants the patient to sit down and have a clear understanding of what is going on. What are they thinking about? What kind of facts come to mind? How do they interpret those facts and what is produced by that interpretation?

They are asked to honestly and accurately say what happens when they think about something, how they feel when they say something, and what they often do when they're feeling certain emotions. The most important aspect of this is the sense of ownership the patient gets.

This thoughts don't come out of nowhere. They're your thoughts. Nobody put them in your brain. Nobody's pointing a gun at your head, demanding that you think those thoughts.

This is the first step— clarity, from which a sense of ownership or control flows. Once the therapist is able to get the patient to admit that this is how they think, they are then in the position to take ownership of how they think.

The next step is to understand that there are two sides of every story. In the first step, we have a clear understanding of what we're thinking about and how we feel about those things. We also have a clear realization of how we interpret facts.

The next step is to look at those facts and see if there are alternative interpretations. For example, you're looking for a job and you send out a hundred resumes, only to get a hundred rejections.

You're thinking to yourself, "I am unemployable. I am a total and complete failure. I'm a loser." Now, please understand that the facts are the same. The fact is you sent out a hundred resumes. The fact is none of those resumes led to a job interview.

Here's the question that the CBT therapist will ask. Given these facts, is the judgement or the conclusion that you are a loser or somehow unemployable the only logical conclusion?

Could it be that you sent out your resume at the end of November and December, where there is a steep drop in employment? Could it be that you're targeting jobs in a particular industry that is seasonal or it is on a downturn?

Could it be that you did no write your resume well enough? Maybe you left out some important details. Maybe you did not have the time to polish your resume. Could it be that you needed a cover letter, instead of just sending out a resume?

When the therapist talks about alternatives this way, you as the patient are forced to look at the facts that you thought were so black and white in a different way. You start getting that, "Aha!" moment.

You start thinking, "Oh okay. I was instantly jumping to the worst conclusion. I was instantly thinking of the worst case scenario." CBT teaches you to become fully aware of your thought process and your conclusions from them.

It doesn't grab you by the neck and say to you, "You're thinking the wrong way. You're thinking negative thoughts or you're thinking about things that you shouldn't be thinking about."

It doesn't do that. Instead, it just puts you in a position to take ownership of what is going on after you are clear about the judgements that you make.

After you are clear about alternative interpretations to the facts of your life, the therapist would coach you how to interpret the same set of facts in a way that pushes you upward or is at least neutral. The ideal is to swap out negative assessments and replace them with positive ones.

If this isn't the case, then at the very worst, the CBT therapist would want you to come up with a neutral conclusion. Another approach would be for the therapist to challenge the patient to look at the past traumatic experience in a different light. How?

The patient is challenged to look for the things that went right. It's very easy to focus only on the things that went wrong. It doesn't take much effort to concentrate on the things that are missing or the areas for improvement.

It does take quite a bit of effort to look at the big picture and understand that there were many other things that were going right. This creates a sense of perspective.

This enables the patient's attitude to change. They start interpreting the experience not from that narrow lens that just focuses on the perceived failure, shortcoming, harm, insult, embarrassment, humiliation, and the negative emotional states at that point in time.

Instead, the person is invited to look at the big picture by paying attention to the things that went right. Everything then falls into place. It doesn't make the hurt go away nor does it make the facts go away, mind you.

However, the patient gets perspective. This enables them to have a healthier frame of mind when it comes to that past trauma. It may well be that as this person got older, the more they exaggerated things in their mind.

It's not unusual for people to have a fairly minor experience in the past. However, given how frustrating their lives have become, they start looking at this past experience as some sort of reason or excuse for why they're struggling in the present day.

This often takes the form of blowing things out of proportion or exaggerating things in your mind. This is the complete process of cognitive behavioral therapy. It's all about changing how you interpret stimuli, either from past memories or information that you are currently receiving.

WHY IS PERSONAL INTERPRETATION SO IMPORTANT?

When you choose how you interpret the neutral stimuli that the world is throwing your way, you are in more control. You can choose an interpretation that makes you feel more confident and enables you to be more effective.

It doesn't have to be the end of the world. The experience you just had doesn't have to be some sort of personal insult. It doesn't have to dismiss you as a total person.

The way you interpret stimuli impacts your emotional state. Your emotional state in turn, impacts what you choose to do. When you go through this process in an unmindful way, you would think that this is all automatic.

You would think that there's really nothing you can do because the moment you start encountering certain things, instinct kicks in. You just end up saying certain things and taking certain actions.

It doesn't have to be that way. You have control over your emotions, your actions, and most importantly your thoughts. You don't have to interpret this memory the exact same way you've been handling out for all these years.

You can choose to change how you interpret. This is the essence of CBT. It's all about changing the mind-set, which leads to a change in attitude and a change in behavior and speech.

These flow into each other. When you make a positive change in how you interpret things, you start acting in a more positive way. This leads to more positive reactions from people around you.

You then feel happier because you are well-received. People are sending you the right signals. This makes it much easier for you to interpret the world in the best possible light.

This then makes you feel emotionally positive, which leads to you taking more effective action. You're doubting yourself less. You're feeling less anxiety. You suffer less depression.

This can create an upward spiral. This is the foundation of cognitive behavioral therapy. It all boils down to how you interpret reality.

CHAPTER 5:

INTERVENTION STEPS PRACTICED BY COGNITIVE BEHAVIORAL THERAPY COUNSELORS AND PROFESSIONALS

As a counselor, these are the steps you have to follow with your client. We'll take the case of depression because this is the most common. If you have a client who is suffering from depression, follow the steps below.

STEP #1: FIND THE PROBLEM AREA IN YOUR LIFE

When somebody's depressed, it's very easy to just say, "I'm depressed." That blanket statement, unfortunately, doesn't really say much. You're just sharing your emotional state.

It's also a clinical diagnosis. It may turn out that you're just sad. Depression, in medical terms, is tightly defined. There's a lot of things that go into depression.

Usually, people use that word very casually. Regardless, the first step is to find the problem areas in your life. What causes this frustration that leads to depression? Is it your relationship? Is it your job or your business?

Does this have something to do with school or health and fitness? Are you having problems with regret? Maybe you feel you picked the wrong spouse. Maybe you think that you are stuck in the wrong job. Regardless, you need to be clear about what parts of your life make you sad or depress you.

STEP #2: BE CONSCIOUS AND AWARE OF YOUR AUTOMATIC THOUGHTS

This is where the robber meets the road. It's easy to say that you have problem areas in your life. Maybe you're stressed out or depressed about not having any money. That part is easy.

You have to look at what triggers your automatic thoughts. Is it that time of the month when you get a big fat envelope from the credit card company with a huge balance? Does it involve your landlord knocking on your door asking for the month's rent?

Whatever the case may be, zero in on what triggers automatic thoughts of depression or extreme sadness. Look for your triggers. This is not always external.

It doesn't have to take the form of a person. It doesn't have to play out as some sort of situation. It can also be a memory.

It's not unusual for people to feel really angry or anxious when an image flashes in their mind. Maybe it's the image of your father who abandoned you as a kid.

Maybe it's an image of an ex who betrayed you by screwing around behind your back. Maybe it's the image of the school bully that humiliated you on a daily basis.

Perhaps it's the face of your boss who love to hate. Maybe it's a very humiliating experience in the past where a lot of kids ganged up on you, beat you up, or laughed at you.

Whatever the case may be, be conscious of your automatic thoughts. Don't automatically assume that just because a certain image flashes in your mind, that there's really only one way to respond.

You may even be thinking that this is the only natural way. It isn't. It's all in your head. You think it's natural, but it turns out that it isn't. It may turn out that you are responding in the least optimal way.

STEP #3: ANALYZE YOUR "AUTOMATIC THOUGHTS"

AND THEIR IMPACT ON YOUR DECISIONS

The cognitive behavioral therapist will first get the patient to lay out what they think automatically. For example, you went through several bad breakups when you were in high school or in college. These really damaged your self-esteem and your self-confidence. They were quite traumatic.

The therapist would then ask you to describe what happened. He or she would then ask you to describe what you think about these memories now and how they impact the way you think, what you talk about, and what you do.

From that point, the therapist would also ask you how your decisions are impacted by your interpretations of these facts.

Through this process, the patient will be the one to realize that the decisions and actions he or she takes may not be all that rational. They may be blowing things out of proportion, they may have lost all perspective, they may be reading too much into what happened in the past, and this is leading them to constantly make the same wrong decisions over and over again.

What's important to note here is that the therapist is not the one making these conclusions. It is not as if this person would say to your face after you tell them what's going on that you are wrong. That's not their job. Their job is to facilitate your self-discovery process so you see the disconnect between how you're judging reality and what you base that judgment on.

You yourself will see the disconnect. You yourself will see that you're drawing all these irrational conclusions from facts. These facts are not going to go away.

Yes, somebody broke your heart. Yes, you got sexually abused. Yes, you got beaten down and physically abused. Those are not going to go away. Facts are facts.

What can go away is the irrational decision or, at the very least, the decisions that you make that are not all that optimal. These decisions continue to hurt you again and again in the here and now.

STEP #4: RECOGNIZE NEGATIVE PATTERNS AND ACTIVELY DISTANCE YOURSELF FROM THEM

The first step to change is not to destroy all negative links. That's too much to ask for. Instead, now that you know where your negative decisions and emotional states are coming from, you need to pay attention to what triggers them.

Pay attention to the almost automatic process of you perceiving something or remembering something, and then feeling negatively. And just as quickly, doing something negative. It's as if you are trying to stop a roller coaster or a runaway train. I'm sure you know that that's almost impossible.

The good news is, by simply being aware of all these connections, you start getting perspective. You start realizing that you don't have to go through the same process that you have habitually gone through. This is the same process that made you feel really lousy at the end.

It doesn't have to end up that way. By understanding how all of these are connected and you start labeling this as something negative, you position yourself to eventually walk away from that old chain reaction.

The first step to creating a better reaction is to recognize, and then put yourself in a position to walk away. This can take quite a while. Don't expect any overnight miracles.

You've been thinking negatively for so long. The negative decisions that you have made have impacted your life profoundly. It would be too much to expect that you would break out of this overnight.

But Step 4 is a significant step because it positions you to have the ability to stop thinking negatively. You're not quite there yet, but this is a turning point.

STEP #5: ACTIVELY COMBAT EVERY UNDERLYING ASSUMPTION YOU MAKE

When you engage in "automatic thinking," you're basically allowing yourself to get carried away by your assumptions. You let them get the better of you.

This doesn't have to be the case. This doesn't have to happen, believe it or not.

One way you can take the power out of this automatic chain reaction is to question the assumptions behind what triggers you. For example, you're walking into a class, and this extremely attractive member of the opposite sex starts laughing in your general direction. As you get closer, that person laughs some more.

The negative interpretation of this scene is so obvious that it doesn't need explanation. You're probably interpreting this in a very negative way. Your assumption is that that person is laughing at you.

Question that assumption. Are there facts that would support that that person is not laughing at you? Pay attention to what's happening in the scene.

Do you remember it clearly? Is somebody whispering to that person's ear and then pointing to himself or herself and making some sort of gesture? It may well be that that person is joking with the person laughing. It can turn out that that person is making a joke of herself or himself.

Believe it or not, that scene that you keep playing in your mind of that personal insult, humiliation and embarrassment might not be all about you. In fact, it might not have anything to do with you. It might have everything to do with the inside joke those two people were sharing.

Question your assumptions because if you don't, this would be invisible. Those details would not exist in your mind. All you see is the person laughing at you. All you can dwell on is your sense of embarrassment and humiliation.

Think of it like a movie scene. You see that person laughing. There's a lot of other people around that person, there's all sorts of commotion, and then there's you walking through the scene.

If you think that that person's actions are all about you, and this was some sort of personal insult, what do you do? Well, you basically crop out the rest of the scene. It's as if everything turns black and white and fades into the background, and the only thing that is in live, vivid color is the person laughing.

That is not a realistic movie. There are many other details out there. Believe it or not, these details provide context, and this context might not lead to the conclusion that you automatically jump to.

Do not be afraid to question your assumptions. Allow yourself to be wrong. Allow yourself to believe that there are alternative explanations. Otherwise, you're going to get hit by that freight train of emotions. It just hits you at full speed and power because you assumed too much.

You might want to knock out its power by looking at your assumptions. It may well turn out that things are not what you think they are. At the very least, you put yourself in a position to interpret the scene in such a way that you are emotionally neutral.

Forget about a positive interpretation. Let's assume that that's not possible. At least shoot for something neutral. You don't have to constantly beat yourself up.

STEP #6: TRY TO SEE THINGS FROM A POSITIVE PERSPECTIVE

Perspective is an art form. It's not a science. Different people can come up with different perspectives. That's just the way it is.

Some people have an instinct or a knack for gaining perspective. They just zoom out and they see the big picture. They see the different pieces of the puzzle.

Other people cannot do that. They dwell on one particular detail and allow it to eat away at them.

Chances are, if you're reading this book, you are more like the latter instead of the former. That's okay. There's no right or wrong answer. What's important is you understand the power of positive perspective and you actively work towards it.

I don't care if you are automatically a negative person, I don't care how long you've been thinking negatively, you have it in you to gain this positive perspective. You just have to claim it. You just have to practice it day after day after day. It takes work.

It's kind of like going to the gym. Remember the first time you hit the weights at the gym? It was murder. No other word would do the experience justice. I mean, your muscles were very flabby and weak and even flat.

When you started lifting weights, you put a lot of pressure on your muscles, and they hurt. But the secret is, when your muscles get sore, that's precisely when you decide to keep going to the gym.

Because your muscles have a memory. And if they absorb all that constant pressure, they quickly tighten. You quickly move out of the soreness phase and your muscles start to fall into place. That's how it works. Don't let the pain throw you off.

The same goes with trying to see events and situations from a positive perspective. There are many different perspectives out there, you're just going to have to identify the positive ones and continue to hammer on them until they become part of your consciousness.

You have to continue picking these until these become your default standard. It is not easy, but it can be done. Just as it isn't easy to go to the gym day after day, even if your body is aching, it can be done. And you would be richly rewarded for it.

STEP #7: DESTROY THE POWER OF THE WORST-CASE SCENARIO

Now that you have the ability to look at things in a more positive perspective, the next step is to understand that the reason why you feel so negatively or you get thrown off is because you always assume the worst-case scenario.

For example, you go to a job interview and the recruiter looks at your resume and then looks at you and gives you a weird look. You can interpret this as essentially signaling that you are unemployable.

You're more than welcome to interpret this as a sign of failure; that you're some sort of unemployable loser. What is the worst-case scenario? That employer will not hire you. So what?

Ask yourself that question. So what? What happens next?

Well, you know what happens next. You go down the list.

There's another employer out there. There are tons of online job sites. There are government jobs. There are jobs in your neighborhood, and other options.

The problem with the worst-case scenario is that it forces you to look at what you're going through as some sort of ultimate disaster. You get into this mindset that there's nothing beyond what's going on in front of you.

But think about it, what is the worst thing that can happen? Your partner leaves you, you get sick, you get fat, you can't get the job or the promotion, you get fired, now what?

When you ask yourself these two questions, you start seeing perspective. You start robbing the worst-case scenario of its tremendous power. These questions, of course, are "Now what?" and "So what?"

Keep asking yourself these questions when you notice that you're entering a negative frame of mind.

When you have identified your assumptions, keep asking these questions. Use them as some sort of battering ram against the deep-seated beliefs that you have about yourself, your competence, your value as a person, and other important beliefs.

You have to understand that these things are only as powerful as you imagine them to be. They draw their power from you.

If you refuse to give them power by constantly asking "So what" and "Now what," you start seeing that there's another world out there. Another world that you can take action on. All is not lost, believe it or not.

STEP #8: WORK BASED ON FACTS

Let's get one thing clear, changing how you think about things takes a lot of work. We also have a lot of fantasies and hopes and wishes regarding our lives.

It's not unusual for people to work based on hopes and wishes and dreams. Some get quite far.

Unfortunately, for most people, this doesn't work. They get stuck in some sort of holding pattern. It's as if they're chasing their tail.

The reason for this is that they're not looking to rebuild their lives and transcend their present realities using facts. This is the key. Base your personal change on reality.

As I mentioned above, facts are facts. You got abused, you got fired unjustly, people slandered you, people hurt you for no good reason, and so and so forth. The list is endless. Now what? So what?

Look at the facts. Are they a complete and total disaster?

For example, your partner left you after several years together, does this mean that it's the end of the world? When you look at the mirror do you see somebody who is just completely unacceptable and so repugnant that nobody in their right mind would want to spend time with you or find value in you?

Of course, not. Look at that fact. That you're still alive, that you can still give, that you can still share. There are just so many things out there. And if you're honest enough, you have a long list of the things that you can offer.

These are facts. They're not going to go away. They're just as solid as the facts of the negative experience or your negative situation. These are the foundation or building blocks of a new perspective.

This is why people who are able to achieve long lasting change in their lives continue to persist because they built the change on facts. They don't build a new life based on what they hope to be true or they assume to be true. That's not going to work.

That's like trying to build a huge structure on sand. It only takes one storm to destroy that building. It's built on sand. Are you building your new life on the sand of wishes and hopes and dreams?

Focus on the facts. Do you have a job? Do you have skills? Can you speak well enough?

These are the types of questions you should ask yourself if you keep coming up with the conclusion that you're unemployable, you'll never ever make money, and other toxic beliefs that hold you back and drag you down from living up to your fullest potential.

Focus on the facts that you have. The fact that you're alive is a big deal. The fact that both your kidneys are working and your lungs are in good shape, those are big deals.

Build your new assumptions and your new perspective on facts. This way, you're realistic. You're not trying to bend reality and insert stuff that doesn't really exist because it's not sustainable.

You're definitely welcome to try, and I'm sure you can achieve some results, but if you really are looking for something sustainable that would withstand the test of time, build on reality. Build on facts.

STEP #9: TAKE OWNERSHIP OF YOUR PERCEPTIONS

In this step, you are going to sum up all the other steps listed above.

In the previous steps, we were just basically isolating the interconnection between facts as they truly exist and your interpretations of them. You are now also fully aware of the impact your interpretations have on the things you think about, how you feel, and your behavior. Now, we're going to take things to a whole other level.

At this point, you know that all these processes are going on. You know, at this point, that your assumptions play a big role in the outcomes you get. At this stage, you're going to take ownership of the whole process. You're going to choose which reality you want for yourself.

This is where judgment comes in. You're going to consciously say, "I know that when I think this way, this is usually what happens. I feel defeated, small, powerless, ugly and hopeless. I know that when I think certain things, it always puts me on that path. This has happened many, many times before."

At this point, your cognitive behavioral therapist would then say, "Do you find other paths?" This is where you start piecing together an alternative.

Please note that you hope that there is a better path. There is an element of wishing here as well.

You obviously wish that there is a better way. You obviously wish for better outcomes. That is obvious. You're not being unrealistic when you do that because that's part of the human condition.

Everybody is drawn to pleasure and tend to shy away from pain. No surprises there. But at this point, your therapist would then work with you to come up with that alternative path.

And by "work with you," I'm not talking about feeding models or plans into your head. They're not doing it right if that's what they're doing. Instead, they prompt you and even challenge you to come up with an alternative.

You know that the way you've always done things leads to negative places. That's a non-starter. So now you're starting over again. Your therapist is then asking you, "What is the better way?"

Come up with a plan. Piece it together. What kind of action steps will you have when certain situations occur?

Maybe it's a past memory, maybe it's a current experience, and maybe it's a predictable pattern that you constantly encounter at work or in some sort of social place. Whatever the case may be, you have to now start coming up with an alternative. This has to be detailed.

You're basically saying to yourself, "Okay, if I say these things one, two and three, I will do x, y and z. I will not do A, B and C. I've been doing A, B and C since forever. Look at me, I'm not happy. I'm not living up to my fullest potential."

You're going to engage in these emotional internal dialogues. It has to be emotional. It has to register at the heart level, otherwise, it's not real.

STEP #10: APPROACH YOUR PERSONAL CHANGE WITH A SENSE OF URGENCY

I've got some bad news for you. I really do. All the information that I've shared here with you is not going to change your life if you do this one thing: keep it in your head.

If you approach the materials that I'm sharing with you from a purely intellectual level, forget about it. Change is not going to happen.

I know that sounds harsh, it might even seem dismissive, but it's true. If you were to look at all the information that I shared with you here and you just file it into your mental cabinets, nothing is going to happen.

You can see the connection, you can see the necessity, you can see the internal logic, you can see patterns, but none of that is going to help you.

It may make all the sense in the world, you may fully understand how cognitive behavioral therapy works, you might have a greater appreciation of the role of the CBT therapist, but your life will continue to remain unchanged.

Why? You did not let it sink into your heart. You did not allow this intellectual information to become emotional information.

People are emotional creatures. We talk a big game about how logical and rational we are. But at the end of the day, we make all sorts of impulsive decisions based on our emotional side.

When we are called out regarding those decisions, that's when our rational side kicks in and we come up with all sorts of seemingly logical explanations for why we made the decisions that we did.

According to a fairly recent psychological research study, consumers were asked regarding their decisions, and it turns out the vast majority actually made the decisions impulsively. But when asked to explain their decisions, they would come up with all sorts of logical or seemingly reasonable explanations.

You have to eventually operate at an emotional level. You have to develop that sense of urgency. Unfortunately, that's not going to happen if you don't let the information that I've shared with you sink to the level of your heart. That's when you will get the drive and the power to keep pushing.

Please understand that what you're doing is very difficult. It really is. It's really hard to change.

We get accustomed to the way we're doing things. Our brains are always looking for the path of least resistance.

Our brains are very powerful and efficient biochemical machines. Once it creates a connection, it's very hard to break that connection. But that's precisely what you need to do.

To get the power to do that consistently over an extended period of time, you need an emotional sense of urgency. This is when you make the transition from viewing cognitive behavioral therapy as a nice little option that you can take if you have the time to something that you must do. This is something that just has to happen, otherwise, you're going to suffer tremendously.

This is how you should think about CBT in your mind. This is how you should frame it. Nothing less will do.

COGNITIVE BEHAVIORAL THERAPY PROGRESSION

What follows is the progression your CBT therapist will step you through to enable you to take fuller control of your thought process and how you take action based on them.

This doesn't have a timeline. Some people can proceed through this list very quickly. Others will take some time.

Everybody's different. No two brains are alike, so don't worry about zipping through this list.

If you are taking much longer, it doesn't mean that there's something wrong with you. It doesn't mean that you are a weak person. It doesn't mean any of that.

Everybody has a different pace. It's perfectly okay if it takes you a long time from point to point. What's important is that you are able to make that journey.

That is what's crucial. Ultimately, the only thing that really matters is that you are taking action on your need to change.

Again, I don't want to repeat myself here, but I need to do it for emphasis. You can read all the information I shared with you here, but until and unless you take action on them, this information is not going to change your life.

You have to act on them. You can't just plug them in your brain and just kick them around like dull, lifeless, intellectual concepts. That's not going to do you any good. You have to take action.

WHAT FOLLOWS IS THE PROCESS:

START WITH A SINGLE THOUGHT

The first thing that you need to do with cognitive behavioral therapy is to zero in on your thoughts on an item by item basis.

Start with one single thought. Pay close attention to how you verbally describe that thought. Are there any loaded words that you are using? Are there any trigger words that you are using? These are emotional words.

For example, there's a big difference between "request" and "demand." There's a big difference between "will" and "may." This may seem small, but if you spot them in how you speak about your thoughts, you learn a lot about your unstated assumptions.

Keep hammering that single thought about yourself. Are there any hidden assumptions? Is it accurate? Is it valid? Does it reflect reality in terms of facts?

EXPOSE ALL ASSUMPTIONS

Now that you have picked away at a single thought that you have about yourself, lay out all the assumptions that this thought depends on.

Assumptions, of course, can vary from the things that you assume that you are perceiving to how you connect what you think you're seeing or perceiving, with things that happened in the past or what will happen in the future.

Lay these all out. There is no right or wrong answer, right off the top of your head. This is a stream of consciousness exercise. Just lay it all out.

Nobody's going to check your work. Nobody should be looking over your shoulder. This is just you. This is private information.

Just lay it out. Don't hold back. You're not going to be offending anybody. You're not going to be letting anybody down. The only person that you're going to disappoint is yourself if you hold back.

So, lay it out. What are you assuming when you think that single thought about yourself?

QUESTION YOUR BELIEFS

Assumptions are beliefs. These are beliefs about what you think are true or how things should be.

Now, using your superior mental processing firepower, hack away at these beliefs. Are these true? Are they true now? Are they going to be true in the future? How good of a job do they do in explaining the past?

How do these beliefs position you? Do they put you in a good light? Do they give you strength? Do they help you become a more effective person?

What kind of facts do they draw on? Are these facts real or are they also assumptions?

In a way, this exercise is similar to taking a ball of string and unwinding it to see smaller knots inside the ball. You unwind those. You take a belief, and you break it apart, and there are smaller beliefs there. Break those apart until you're left with your assessment of reality.

Now, at this stage, you're going to say to yourself, is this accurate or are there alternative interpretations? If it's accurate, does it hurt me? If it hurts me, are there alternative applications that will at least make the overall effect neutral?

When you do this, you see how your beliefs have been distorted. Maybe you're blowing things out of proportion. Maybe you are not looking at the actual facts.

BE SURE YOUR PERSONAL FACTS ARE REALLY FACTS

I know that the subheading title is kind of confusing. But the truth is, when we look at past events in our lives, we often read into them elements that actually arose from later issues in our lives.

It's like a historian going through a war, rewriting history of a battle that took place in the distant past. In this rewrite, all the hopes, dreams, wishes of that historian's society in the here and now is projected onto the past. So, when students in the future will read that historical narrative of a battle that's supposed to have happened a long, long time ago, it actually speaks to the values and objectives of a later date.

Historians do this all the time. Political commentators do this. Politicians definitely do this. And, believe it or not, people living their individual lives do this when it comes to their personal histories.

Well, doing this obviously serves a very important purpose. It gives you a sense of direction. It gives you a sense of meaning. But the problem is, you have to be aware that you're doing this, and you also have to be aware that, ultimately, it's lying.

Facts are facts. Interpretations are interpretations. Know the difference. Know where to draw the line.

This is why you have to look at the facts that you think exists in your life and break them up. Is this really what happened? Are there gaps? Is the timeline correct or has it been shrunk? Has it been pasted together and fused with stuff that happened later on?

This is especially true when it comes to experiences of abuse.

A lot of clinical psychologists and counselors got into a lot of trouble in the past because they were asking the wrong questions to their patients. These questions were loaded. They were not neutral. They did not lay out a neutral platform for the patient to hash out his or her issues.

Instead, they were loaded questions. There were assumptions in them. And it's no surprise that the patient started filling in the assumptions.

If you want to see a horrific example of this, look up the case of the McMartin Day Care. In that case, government social workers interviewed kids regarding sexual molestation and abuse in a day care center.

The questions they asked essentially coached the kids to give the answers the investigators were looking for. This resulted in a series of indictments of people that ran the day care.

It turns out that the kids were basically trying to please the people interviewing them. So, when the interviewee said, "Did this person touch you?" or "How did this person touch you?" all these horrific details would come out. It turns out that this was all imagined information to fit the questions.

You may be doing the same with yourself. You may be reading in all sorts of issues into past facts. And the more you do this, the more hardwired those facts seem. They seem really immovable because, hey, I believed them for so long.

Well, now is the time to take a sledgehammer and start blasting away at the things that you assume are facts. This doesn't take much effort.

You don't have to have a graduate degree to do this. You just basically have to ask the journalists' six questions: who, what, where, when, why and how.

Here's a pro tip: do not start with why. Focus on everything else first. You will quickly find out that a lot of the facts that you have automatically assumed were true are actually spotty at best.

There might be certain key elements missing, but you still assume that this is the truth. But it's missing a key element, and that key element is actually what would justify you making all these negative conclusions based on these facts.

If you were to plug in those missing parts, these facts may well support a completely different conclusion. This is how you know that your beliefs are distorted. You don't have to put yourself through this process.

UNDERSTAND THE POWER OF MOOD

Please understand that when you're looking at past facts and you're trying to make an analysis or you're trying to judge what happened in the past, they're dependent on how you feel at that given point in time.

A lot of people discount this. They think, "Well, facts are facts. I just need to think about certain things and the explanation and the conclusion pretty much jumps out at me. It doesn't take much effort. It's smooth and it flows just like water."

Fine, you can feel that way. But understand that your mood at that time actually impacts how easy it would be for you to accept that conclusion.

And when you're in the same mood when you think about that fact over and over again, you become blind to the fact that you are analyzing that fact in the worst way.

Pay attention to your mood when you think of certain things and situations. For example, when you're feeling lonely and you think about your ex-girlfriend and how she lied to you, cheated on you, took money from you, what kind of facts do you think you will draw? What do you focus on? What kind of facts do you think you will become blind to?

Do you see how this works? Pay attention to your mood. Your

mood might actually be putting you in a situation where you will constantly draw the wrong conclusions.

Now, let's flip the script. Let's say you're in a happy mood because you met somebody new. She's so awesome compared to all the women you've been with. Do you think about your ex-girlfriend at that point?

Probably not. You're in a good mood. You feel like you're on top of the world. Do you see how this works?

Do not neglect the importance of mood. It actually plays a bigger role than you think.

CHAPTER 6:

CBT BEST PRACTICES

Please take note of the following best practices. If you are seriously considering going through cognitive behavioral therapy, make sure that the therapist you're working with has the following best practices in place. If not, ask them if you can do the following. Whatever the case may be these best practices can help you get better results from your CBT therapy sessions. These therapy sessions do not have to involve face to face therapists.

You can do it online. You can go through some sort of assisted program. Whatever the case may be, there has to be an expert at the other side of the equation. You can't do this alone. That person must have the proper experience to guide you through the process so you can get optimal results.

Now, keep in mind that this is not a race. You're not trying to get from point A to point B as quickly as possible. The only person that is setting the pace of your progress is yourself. Take your time. You're trying to rebuild your life. Your life is built on your thoughts. You are your thoughts. And just as you can choose your thoughts, you can choose your life.

There's an old quote attributed to the ancient Chinese philosopher Confucius. It goes something like this, "If you sow a thought, you reap a word. When you sow a word, you reap an action. When you sow an action, you reap a habit. When you sow a habit, you reap a character. When you sow a character, you reap a destiny."

There's a lot of truth to this saying. Ultimately, you choose your destiny. How? On the surface, it's kind of mind-blowing because a destiny is huge, it's big, it takes forever. It's a work of a lifetime. It also has far-reaching impact.

Well, it all begins with the thoughts that you choose on a moment to moment basis. Just as a mighty river starts out as a tiny stream. Your destiny, as vast as it may be starts with a single thought. Those tiny streams that make up the White Nile flow together until it forms the Nile River. The same can be said about the Amazon River in Brazil.

It all has to start somewhere. Believe it or not, it starts out small. If you're not paying attention, you might not even notice. But if you take ownership of your thoughts and you actively choose them with the full understanding that they lead to somewhere big, and you choose your ultimate destination based on something big, you then put yourself in a situation where you are choosing your ultimate destination by choosing your thoughts in the here and now. The following best practices help you to do this.

DOCUMENT EVERYTHING

You should keep a journal that tracks your cognitive behavioral therapy progress. It doesn't have to be anything fancy. It doesn't have to have all sorts of graphs and charts. It doesn't have to have any of that. Instead, it can be just a simple diary. What is important is the date and the thoughts that you log. Even if you only have time for a few sentences, that's okay. As long as you are clear regarding your thoughts and your perceptions of those thoughts.

That's all you need to do because when you sit down with your therapist, you go through this material and you see your progression. You also able to pinpoint the impact of your mood or anything else that may be happening in your life and how it is reflected and how you judge your thoughts.

You should also track how your thoughts lead to action. What kind of actions do you normally take? Are you happy with those actions? Are there alternative paths you could have taken? Where do these lead back to? What kind of thoughts can these be traced back to? This journal is not only a diary but it is also a passport to a new life.

EXPOSE YOURSELF TO CHALLENGES

One of the most common reasons people undergo CBT involves phobias. They're afraid of going out into an open space where there are a lot of other people. They're afraid of meeting new people. They're afraid of spiders. They're afraid of heights, and so on and so forth. For CBT to work, you have to put pressure on your cognitive behavioral muscles. This means that you are going to make yourself uncomfortable. You can't just stand one thousand feet away from whatever it is that is stressing you out or causing all sorts of anxiety and depression and try to make changes. It doesn't work that way. This is just an intellectual exercise. You're just wasting your time if that's your attitude.

You have to get in the middle of things. You have to jump in. You have to feel it. You have to feel uncomfortable. You have to step out of your comfort zone. Now, this doesn't mean that you're going to put yourself in harm's way, don't overdo it. What this does mean, is that you have to allow yourself to be transformed by actual real-life experiences.

These gives you opportunities to carry-out the information that I have taught you so far. Without this valuable practice, you're just wasting your time. You might as well go to graduate school where you read case studies. Those case studies are actual businesses. They actually make or lose money. They have real flesh and blood human employees. Those are case studies, they're real. But you're dealing with them in an unreal way. You're dealing with them in a cold antiseptic secure place. You're dealing with them in an intellectual way. Well, if you want this stuff that you've read in this book, to truly help you change your life and turn things around, you have to put them into action.

You have to expose yourself to things that you fear. You have to intentionally put yourself into situation where you may become uncomfortable. And that's perfectly okay because it feels so much better when you overcome your fear. That's where you gain a sense of accomplishment. You've done something big. You have overcome.

AVOID FAKE SUBSTITUTES

There are sorts of fake substitutes to the mental and emotional heavy lifting you should be doing to get out from under your unhealthy personal assumptions. This can take many forms. Maybe you go to fortune tellers, maybe you watch a lot of YouTube videos of people doing all sorts of mentalist tricks. Those are not going to help you. They really not. Palm readers can tell you what you want to hear but all they are doing is giving you a false sense of hope. The hope here is that somehow, someway have some sort of control over your future.

Well, the only way to do that is to get out from under the negative assumptions you have about your past which push you to make all sorts of negative interpretations in the here and now. These have a real effect because you take the wrong actions again and again and again. When you try to gain some sense of control about the future by talking to a fortune teller or reading horoscopes you're just numbing yourself. That's all you're doing. That's like taking drugs instead of dealing with depression.

That's like drinking a lot of coffee when you should be working on the project. You're just drinking coffee and reading. That's not helping you. You have to drink coffee and work. Stay away from false substitutes, as I said this can take many different forms. It can also take the form of your family, believe it or not.

If you know that you have to make serious career changes and you have to work on turning your income-generating abilities around, one common tactic people take is to just shift almost all their time to their family. On the surface this is awesome. I mean this is crucial because, at the end of the day, your loved ones must take priority. But the problem is you're overdoing it. You're using it as a form of escape.

Believe it or not, you're not doing them any favors because they are relying on you. You may not end up giving them the life that they deserve because you're afraid to confront your fears. For whatever reason, you don't want to step out of the shadow of your past and you always holds you back and drags you down from living up to your fullest potential. Who do you think suffers?

Obviously, it going to be you but it's also were to be people who depend on you. Do not use your family as a crutch. That's the worst thing you can do to them. They're relying on you. They want you to be the best version of you. Unfortunately, the only person that can do that is you.

USE WORKAROUNDS TO SPEEDUP CBT'S EFFECTS

There are certain simple tricks that you can use to speed up the effects of the CBT. You can prepare yourself by asking yourself some stock questions. Whenever you feel triggered by let's say a negative memory, ask yourself, "Am I assuming too much? Is this the only interpretation? Am I seeing all the facts here? What am I basing this on? I know that this leads to something bad. Am I basing this on reality? Are there alternative conclusions to this?"

Come up with your own question. Come up with the question that really cuts you to the heart. Everybody's different so we tend to phrase our questions differently so it's okay. But come up with your own version that grabs your attention. You want to come up with a series of questions that stops you on your tracks when you otherwise could be riding that emotional rollercoaster and there is no stopping it.

You get triggered, you start assuming all the worst things and then you feel really bad and then you end up making a decision that you regret later on. This happens again and again and again, becomes a habit. You feel that this is just part of you. There's nothing you can do to change it. That's not true, that's a lie. Wake up to the lie.

Do yourself a big favor, come up with packed questions. These are canned questions that you always come back to so you can arrest, freeze, stop or thwart that rollercoaster that starts with your thoughts.

As I mentioned in a previous chapter, the world is essentially neutral. It's sending you all sorts of neutral signals. It's up to you to make the interpretation. It's the interpretation that counts more than the stimuli. Your interpretation can make your life heaven or hell. Guess what? It all turns on your ability to respond. Take ownership of that. Don't feel that you're just watching this movie that's going to play out regardless of what you do or regardless of how you feel.

That's a powerless way of looking at your life. And you look at that movie, please understand that you write the script. You direct the cameras. You edit whatever shows up on the screen. And most importantly, you act in it. You play all the roles believe it or not. Take ownership of this process by having a ready-list of questions that stop the flow or the speed at which you make interpretations. Get out from under generalization, assumptions or irrelevant thoughts that have always held you back.

STOP BLAMING OTHERS

What if I told you that the moment you blame other people you are handing them control over your life. Now, you might be thinking this is illogical. After all, these people actually caused you harm. They actually did something negative to you. Now you're going to ask me not to blame them? Well, think of it this way. While it's true that these people are the actual practical and logical cause of what happened to you, how you respond to that fact can hold you back and keep you down. It can prevent you from living a life full of possibility and power.

How? Well, you keep blaming them. Sure, they actually caused the problem but your response is not optimal. It doesn't lead to a sense of possibility. It doesn't lead to a sense of power. Why? Simple logic, if somebody is to blame for whatever happened to you, then they also have the solution, the fix. They can fix it because they caused it. This is how your internal logic works. You may not be aware of it but it's there.

Accordingly, you don't have to change. This is the big reward the people really are shooting for when they blame. These two are interlinked by assigning the blame to somebody else or situation beyond your control, you also give them the power to change things. This also has a matching effect on you because it freezes you from the responsibility of having to lift a finger to change your situation.

Sure you got abused in the past, sure you got cheated, embarrassed, humiliated, degraded, you name it. Those happen. Those people are logically to blame. Now what? So what? You'll have to live your life here and now. Those people have moved on. That ex-girlfriend that cheated on you and took your money, she has a family now. She's a Born-again Christian, she's happy, she's moved on. But you're still miserable. That boss that you felt degraded you in that meeting has become a billionaire. He's moved on.

But my question to you is, are you ready to move on or you going to continue to give them the power to change your life? Because that's what you're really doing. You're equating the logical cause of whatever hurt you in the here and now with the ability to turn things around. Well, you need to split that up. You really do. Yes, those people in those situations are to blame. Yes, you had a bad childhood. Yes, your father left you when you're two years old, abandoned you. Yes, your Mama abused you.

It doesn't matter. Those are in the past. They did cause those things. But the responsibility for your life lies squarely with you.

Take ownership of that responsibility. You can't get those people to come back and fix your life, that's just not going to happen. You can't jump into some sort of time machine to go back and reverse what happened. You have to change how you respond now because when you do that you claim the power of turning your life around.

You also reject the cheap reward that you get of irresponsibility. This doesn't get you off the hook. Get used to it. Is it unfair? Absolutely! Does it suck? You're right. But it's your responsibility. Take ownership right here, right now. Stop blaming. It's not going to do anybody one bit of good.

STOP PERSONALIZING

One of the most common issues people are confronted with is when they look at situations that happen in the past and they personalize them. For example, they made a mistake but they personalize this as "The Loser." So they put their name, let's say your name is Joe Blow, the Loser. If you find yourself doing this, stop personalizing. That is not Joe Blow. Your past does not define you. So you cheated, you lied, you screwed around on your girlfriend or boyfriend but that doesn't have to define you. That was you in a given time and in a given place. Forgive yourself. Let go of that because you're more than that.

Believe it or not, there are lots of beautiful, good, kind and loving people in this world who have done really horrible stuff. They have abused kids, they've abused drugs, they've stolen, they've lied, they've broken all sorts of laws, and they manipulated people.

SO WHAT? NOW WHAT?

Keep asking those two questions because when you ask them in this context you quickly realize that your past does not have to define you. Your crimes are not the only source of your identity. Your sins do not make up your complete moral DNA as a person.

You see where I'm coming from? Good. Take ownership of this. Understand that who you are is a choice and it's a choice made moment by moment.

It all boils down to the thoughts you choose. It all boils down to your analysis of what you have perceiving because if you want a better destiny for yourself then pay attention to how your choices of thoughts lead to that destiny. You may have come from a family of drug addicts, sex addicts, prostitutes, pimps, criminals, it doesn't matter. You are in control of your life.

Do not let anybody fool you into thinking you don't have that control. This is basic responsibility and self-ownership. Step up.

Unfortunately, when you personalize past failures and say, "Ah that's Joe Blow The Loser, that's me," you're dooming yourself. You're making yourself out some sort of flat two-dimensional cartoon. You're not just a series of actions. Maybe that was just you in the past. That was a particular point in time. Maybe you are hooked on heroin. So what? You can get off that habit. You can turn your life around. You can face your fear straight in the eye and overcome that fear and become a better person. And guess what happens, nobody has the right to dismiss you. Because if anything you are better than them.

They didn't have to overcome a childhood of abuse. They didn't have to overcome heroin addiction. They didn't have to overcome being a prostitute or being trafficked. You have to walk a mile in your shoes. Who are they to judge you? Please understand that the worst judge of your character that you will ever face is yourself. So judge right. Your past does not have to define you. Stop personalizing. Stop reducing yourself into a series of mistakes and bad judgments.

ADOPT MINDFULNESS

There are many mindfulness methods you can adopt so you can become more perceptive of your thoughts. Can be very formal. I am of course talking about meditation. Meditation is thousands of years old and there are many different "flavors" of meditation. Some are mystical and religious than others. A lot have a specific spirituality that they are closely associated with. Others are more stripped down. They're focused more on how your mind works.

Whatever the case may be, pick a form of mindfulness that you can stick to consistently. It can be something as basic as breathing deeply and then stopping for five seconds and then breathing out and then stopping for five seconds and then repeating this process until you're fully relaxed. You can also try present sense mindfulness where you basically just look at something in front of you. Right now, I'm looking at a fan. So I'd look straight at the middle of the fan and focus all my perception on it.

Eventually, I'm not seeing anything else and just seeing the fan and its' background. I freeze my thoughts. This is the essence of mindfulness because mindfulness really is all about training yourself to focus on the present moment. In any given second you're thinking about all sorts of stuff. You're thinking about the rent that has to be paid, you're thinking about driving your kids to soccer practice, you're thinking about ordering a latte from Starbucks, you're thinking about a million things.

When you practice mindfulness you unclench. It's as if you went from carrying many different shopping bags to dropping everything and just focusing on that one small envelope in front of you. It doesn't matter how you do it. You can count your breath, you can acknowledge your thoughts, you can use a mantra, and you can practice visualization. There are a million and one ways to get to the same place. What's important is that you get there. Because this ability enables you to focus on the truth of your thoughts which lead you to become a better analysis of your personal reality.

With this skillset, you become a more relaxed person. You're able to divorce your emotions from your thoughts. Just because certain things are happening around you doesn't mean that you have to react in the worst way possible. You may have done that in the past but that doesn't mean that you have to do it now.

Keep these best practices in mind because they go a long way in helping you get out from under the negative interpretations that are making you suffer. You have to understand and remember that these are interpretations. You're the one making the interpretation. You are always in control. Take full ownership and responsibility of this ability and you will start living a better life. There's nobody else to blame except yourself. There is no better time than now. Do it. You owe it to yourself and your loved ones.

CONCLUSION

Cognitive behavioral therapy has helped countless people through the years overcome fears, anxieties, and negative mental habits that kept them from living a happier, more fulfilling life. CBT can help you too... if you let it.

The information you read in this book is not self-executing. You can't just read this book and all of a sudden, your life starts to improve. CBT doesn't work that way.

Oftentimes, recovery can be an uncomfortable if not painful process. How come? We have to overcome our mental habits. We have to purposefully change the way we look at life, ourselves, and how we view our personal capabilities. This means overcoming fear, dealing with pride, and committing to confronting our personal issues right in the eyes...

The good news? The more you practice CBT-regardless of how low level your starting point may be-the better you'll get at it. You'll grow in confidence and you'll be able to achieve better and better results. It all boils down to choosing to start right now. Right here.

I wish you nothing but the best in your quest for a happier, more fulfilling, more meaningful life.